CHINESE COUNTRY ANTIQUES:
VERNACULAR FURNITURE AND ACCESSORIES

c. 1780-1920

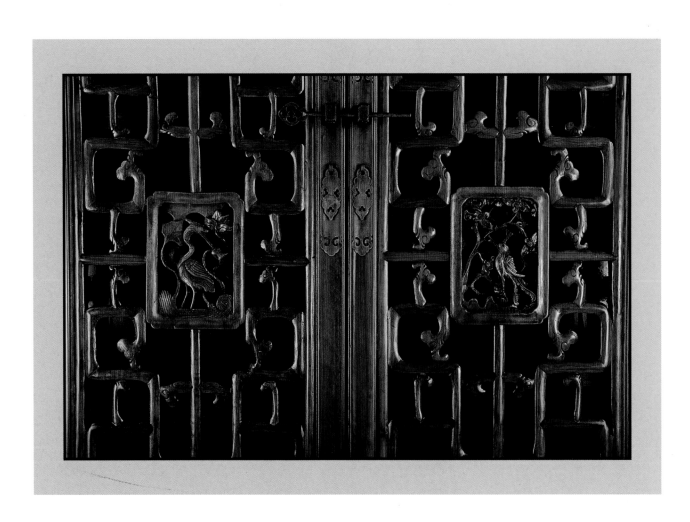

CHINESE COUNTRY ANTIQUES:

VERNACULAR FURNITURE AND ACCESSORIES

c. 1780-1920

Revised 2nd
Edition

Schiffer Publishing Ltd

4880 Lower Valley Road, Atglen, PA 19310 USA

Andrea & Lynde
McCormick

Revised price guide: 2002
Copyright © 2000 & 2002 by Andrea & Lynde McCormick

Library of Congress Cataloging-in-Publication Data
McCormick, Andrea.
   Chinese country antiques : vernacular furniture and accessories,
c. 1780-1920 / Andrea and Lynde McCormick. -- Rev. 2nd ed.
       p. cm.
   ISBN: 0-7643-1585-4
   1. Furniture--China. 2.Furniture--Collectors and collecting. I.
   McCormick, Lynde. II. Title.
   NK2668.M38 2002
   749.2951--dc21
                              2002002139

Cover design by Bruce Waters
Book designed by Blair Loughrey
Type set in Albertus Medium/Korinna/Zurich

ISBN: 0-7643-1585-4
Printed in China
1 2 3 4

Published by Schiffer Publishing Ltd.
4880 Lower Valley Road
Atglen, PA 19310
Phone: (610) 593-1777; Fax: (610) 593-2002
E-mail: Schifferbk@aol.com
Please visit our web site catalog at
www.schifferbooks.com

This book may be purchased from the publisher.
Include $3.95 for shipping.
Please try your bookstore first.
We are interested in hearing from authors
with book ideas on related subjects.
You may write for a free catalog.

In Europe, Schiffer books are distributed by
Bushwood Books
6 Marksbury Ave.
Kew Gardens
Surrey TW9 4JF England
Phone: 44 (0) 208 392-8585; Fax: 44 (0) 208 392-9876
E-mail: Bushwd@aol.com
Free postage in the U.K., Europe; air mail at cost.

CONTENTS

FOREWORD

It was early evening, and Hong Kong's dramatic, harbor side skyline was just beginning to light up. Boats still churned back and forth in the harbor, and what should have been a pleasant dinner with friends had just slipped into an awkward silence.

A look of concern and frustration crossed the face of Barbara Acton Bond, as she stopped mid-sentence and looked at her husband.

We had just asked to take her up on an offer to share her business sources with us, and she had just realized that she may have made the offer in regrettable haste. The Acton Bonds were an American/British couple who had lived in Hong Kong for more than 10 years, she as an antique dealer. She had the best sources in Hong Kong, an important resource in a business that can bring out more than a little larceny in a lot of people. They all regarded Barbara with the utmost respect.

They were dear friends, and she had, in a moment of friendship, offered to share those sources and her considerable knowledge of Chinese antiques with us. Now, over dinner, she wasn't so sure.

The problem, weighed in her husband, was that she had made the same offer to another close friend who promptly used the information to become a competitor. Barbara's main line of business – in addition to buying and selling antiques – was taking Western visitors on antique shopping trips in Hong Kong. She took them to the best dealers, got the best deals, and was paid for it. Her friend had become so taken with the antiques that she succumbed to temptation and used Barbara's years of experience and expertise to start her own business.

Barbara was understandably wary of the same treatment from us.

From our point of view, the prospect seemed impossible. We had a modest interest in antiques, less of an interest in Chinese furniture, and were well entrenched in our own careers. Lynde had been a journalist for 25 years and was working in Hong Kong as an anchor for CNBC-TV, the American business news channel that launched a network in Asia. Andrea was happy with her career in early childhood education and enjoyed a wonderful position as general manager of six preschools in Hong Kong, with 500 children and a staff of about 100.

We assured Barbara that we were only interested in her field as a possible hobby and another way to learn about Chinese culture.

So she relented and consented to show us the inside track of her business. And what a business! She showed us furniture we had never seen or even imagined, design that was so exciting it stopped us in our tracks. We soon shucked both our careers to become antique dealers. Let me quickly point out that we not only approach the business from a different angle – we import Chinese furniture, accessories, and artifacts and do not take customers on shopping trips – but we started our business with Barbara. We parted ways professionally when Barbara moved back to England but remain close friends. She still deals in Chinese antiques, although with a focus on artifacts.

What she showed us took us by surprise. We had arrived in Hong Kong with no fondness for Chinese design, believing, like many Americans, that it was too stylized – highly ornate carving on ebony-colored wood. And while that is true for some, it is not true for a new genre of antiques that has only just become available to Westerners. What we saw was fun, serious, colorful, elegant, simple, complex, rustic, and refined – and unbelievably low-priced. It knocked our socks off. We initially bought some pieces for our own collection with no thought of becoming antique entrepreneurs.

When we returned to the U.S. in 1997, we essentially returned to our original careers and planned to stay with them.

But China gets under your skin. We wanted to maintain contacts with Asia as well as expand our appreciation of Chinese culture. We also started to think that other Americans would be as enthusiastic about this furniture as we were.

Within a month of our return, Andrea decided to start a business importing late Qing (Ching) dynasty furniture and selling it at antique shows, primarily in the northeast. Lynde helped out and, after 2-1/2 years, joined the company full time.

Our interest was as much cultural and historical as it was a love of beautiful things and an appreciation of extraordinary craftsmanship. We searched out and read everything we could on the subject, visited museums, and sought out experts in the U.S. and China.

We found the customer excitement we had expected, and our own enthusiasm and love for these pieces has continued to grow.

Read just a few chapters or even paragraphs of this book, and you will have no doubts about where we stand on Chinese furniture from the late Qing dynasty. We love it. We find it to be imaginative and beautiful. We believe that, well chosen, it enhances most design schemes. We even prefer it to the classical Chinese furniture that occupies such lofty ground in the preferences and pocketbooks of more traditional collectors.

But we are obviously not the only collectors of late Qing furniture, nor the only company selling it. The field is full, and it is also full of questionable quality. This book seeks three goals to help buyers negotiate the traffic:

To provide an introduction to people who are unfamiliar with the pieces, people who, like us, thought they did not like Chinese furniture and would never own a piece. We hope to share our excitement over finding the most beautiful, the most extraordinary furniture we have ever seen, at remarkably low prices.

To provide an overview of the genre. Lots of our customers have seen Chinese pieces but know very little about them – their history, construction, finishes, provenance, and importance.

To provide a brief buying guide. Quality varies widely, from wedding cabinets you can buy for $500 on the street corners in New York's Chinatown to exquisite pieces that sell for thousands under the gavel at auction houses. Prices also vary, from the high-end shops in New York and Hong Kong to some Asian treasure you might dig up at one of the giant flea markets around the U.S.

We've attempted to carve out the middle ground in our price ranges. You may well find a lower price on similar pieces, and you will certainly be able to find higher prices. If you find a pair of horseshoe back armchairs at a shop on the East Side of New York priced at $5,000 – a distinct possibility – don't count on bargaining the dealer down to the $2,000 cited in this book. And don't storm out of the shop thinking you're being exploited. Save that move for the $10,000 chairs – also a distinct possibility.

Successful antique shopping involves seeing something you like, deciding whether the price is reasonable, and deciding what you can afford. If the answer comes up "yes" to all of the above, our consistent advice in this book is to go for it. You may never find such a piece again. Our goal is to help you decide what constitutes a reasonable price for commensurate quality.

We also want to let you know that, we believe, *prices will* rise sharply on these pieces, perhaps in as soon as five years. China, as a country, is unloading this furniture – shipping it out and flooding the market. All the demand is in the West, making China a pure source. Eventually, the supply will slow and perhaps stop – either because of a newly discovered cultural awareness in China or because the pipeline has run dry. Demand has already started to increase in China, for example, which has seen record prices paid for individual pieces.

As a final note, it's important to realize that there are no absolutes in these, or any, Chinese antiques. It's a big country with a long history and a great variety of cultural expression. Any attempt to produce a definitive set of rules is doomed to death by a thousand cuts. One expert can insist, for example, that the tops of certain types of tables must have a beaded border to be authentic. Another expert will dismiss that claim as "utter nonsense." Both perspectives may well be legitimate. Contradictions and disagreements can be as sharp as the example cited here and as subtle as preferences of taste.

They stem in part from the diversity of furniture from the late Qing. Some pieces were made to imitate court furniture, but many more came from villages, towns, cities, and provinces far removed the capital city. They were made by craftsmen who followed their own sense of design – their own sensitive vision and inspiration – not the dictates of the Imperial court. These pieces were made for both the elegant activities of a wealthy merchant class as well as every day living and working for traders, merchants, druggists, accountants, etc.

So a table with straight, horse hoof legs that have been chiseled out with a rough touch may have as much charm as one whose legs gently taper into a more refined horse hoof.

The ornamentation that makes a cabinet or box appealing to a Western decorator may have been considered vulgar by furniture Poobahs of that time… and this.

It is this wide range of creative license, of personality, that makes these antiques so appealing to us and, we suspect, you. Visit the classical, Ming dynasty Chinese furniture exhibits at museums from Boston's Fine Arts to Kansas City's Nelson Atkins, and you'll see wonderful pieces that look very much the same from venue to venue. Tables, cabinets, and chairs frequently share much the same heritage of design.

But browse the wares of dealers who sell pieces from the late Qing dynasty, and you'll find some similarity as well as numerous one-of-a-kind treasures, full of individual and cultural stories and history.

HISTORY

Not the Black Sideboard You Got from Grandma

Try to imagine all the antique furniture of Europe, the culmination of centuries of taste and design ... unwanted in Europe. It is owned by farmers and clerks and schoolteachers. They, however, feel little or no cultural attachment to it.

Then all of a sudden, antique dealers from the United States and South America start clamoring for it. They show up with their checkbooks and go home with container loads. The Europeans cannot believe their good fortune. They are much more interested in raising some cash – to continue a child's education or buy a new TV – than in connecting with the past, especially one currently in official disfavor. And here come these peculiar foreigners willing to pay top dollar for their beat up sticks of wood.

The Europeans start unloading their antiques just as fast as new buyers show up and at prices that seem generous to them but bargain-basement to the Americans.

Implausible as it may seem, this is the situation that burst upon the Western antiques market in the 1990s, but with Chinese, not, obviously, European antiques. Western collectors had "discovered" a new variety of antiques in the 1980s as China opened up to outsiders for the first time in decades. These newly found antiques, 100-300 years old, were elegant, rustic, refined, simple, complex, whimsical, serious – all the elements that make for a comprehensive genre. And with little domestic demand for it in China, this furniture began to flow to American and European markets.

Historically, this is important furniture. It comes from the final years of the Qing (Ching) dynasty, the last dynasty in China's long, long history of rule by emperors, and it represents, quite literally, the end of a cultural continuity that persisted uninterrupted for thousands of years. China was unified under a single emperor in 221 BC and more or less stayed that way until 1911.

The Qing dynasty, which started in 1644, was not just the final dynasty, but one that brought with it a new cultural dynamic. It was under the Qing emperors that the Westerners first challenged the concept of China as the Middle Kingdom, and as their influence grew, their ideas and tastes both mixed and clashed with those of China. It was also under the Qing emperors that a new, wealthy merchant class rose to prominence and wanted homes and furnishings in accord with their status. Unlike the ruling elite,

whose tastes had dominated design for centuries, these new consumers did not feel constrained by imperious rules about how furniture should and should not look. What they demanded was something quite different from traditional Chinese design. What they produced was something more energetic than traditional Western ideas about Chinese decor.

It is often called *vernacular* furniture, a term popularized by Nancy Berliner in her book "Friends of the House," the most comprehensive work, to date, on furniture made for ordinary Chinese, the so-called *lin bao* (the original 100 surnames of Chinese population.)

The term "vernacular," though, is problematic in that it carries a range of meanings. It has only entered the lexicon of Western terms to describe Chinese culture within the last 10 years. With a broad brush, it describes Chinese society outside the imperial court, whose cultural sphere of influence extended out from the capital city. And it was a pervasive influence that settled over thousands of court members and their families. Cultural activities and decorative arts of imperial China followed rigid rules and have been the focus of Western study of China. But there was life outside the court, and it was marked by regional creativity that ranged from conservative to flamboyant. "Vernacular" as a cultural marquee has come to describe this non-imperial China.

But those parameters cover a lot of ground, from three-room peasant homes to enormous mansions with multiple dwellings and courtyards within their walls. When applied to furniture, the term tends to suggest rustic, simple, ordinary – furniture that was, and still is, used in farm homes and peasant villages. It was purely practical but nonetheless draws on centuries of design patterns and refinement that give it a sense of charm and grace.

At the other end of the scale is furniture made as luxury items for merchants with wealth of stunning proportions.

Some dealers use the vernacular moniker to cover the whole ground. Others distinguish between city and country furniture, the former being more refined. Some, like us, fly the "country antiques" banner, a suggestion of country furniture from Europe and the U.S. Still others call it provincial furniture, because it was made for owners who lived in the provinces of China rather than the capital city.

Whatever its nomenclature, it is wonderful stuff, vastly different from the highly ornate, ebony colored pieces your grandparents may have acquired during travels to Taiwan or pre-Mao China. This "in between' furniture of the late Qing dynasty is the focus of this book. It was fine furniture made for a merchant class that reached its economic zenith, if not social prominence, for the first time during the 18th century.

It marks a brilliant departure from what you might have read about in books or seen in museums, the *classical* style so closely associated with Chinese pieces.

It's colorful. It's creative. It's too fine to lump in with the more rustic vernacular and too expressive to fall under the shadow of classical design. This book seeks to give antique collectors, dealers, and buyers an informed introduction and overview to the furniture and accessories from the late Qing dynasty of the 18th and 19th centuries.

It is often furniture that has been colored – red, black, burgundy, purple – or painted with scenery and designs. In that respect it differs sharply from perceptions of classical furniture, which is usually considered – inaccurately as it turns out – to have a natural wood finish.

A number of collectors consider the clear, hardwood finishes of classical Ming furniture to represent the pinnacle of Chinese furniture making. But

this seems a largely Western sentiment, rooted in a persistent theme of Sino superiority that colors Western perspectives on China from the early 18th to early 20th centuries. The simple lines and natural finishes of Ming hardwood furniture were considered evidence of an austere elegance and moral superiority in Chinese culture.

But it was a preference not shared by the Chinese, who apparently placed greater value on colored and painted furniture. This marks an important distinction for collectors of late Qing furniture, because painted furniture requires a different kind of wood than that used for the Ming classical furniture.

Ming and early Qing nobles apparently preferred a wood called *zitan*, grown in Southeast Asia and imported to China. It was extremely hard and lent itself to thin, graceful structural members – legs, arm rests, chair rails, and corner posts, etc. It was so prized by the upper classes, that they cut it to extinction.

The other wood long associated with classical Ming furniture was *huanghuali*, found primarily on the south China island of Hainan. Also quite dense, it has a tight grain and honey-colored hue and was also thought, until recently, to have been cut to extinction.

The grains on these hard woods generally were too tight to hold a color. That task fell to softer woods,

such as the southern and northern elm which dominate pieces from the late Qing. There is some thinking among collectors that furniture makers of the period turned to the softer woods because the hardwoods were all but gone. But one might just as easily conclude that only the softwoods were capable of expressing the creative forces that spurred on these craftsmen and their patrons.

As you read this book, an important word to keep in mind is "whimsical." We might not always associate China with whimsy, especially since Mao, but a subtle sense of humor weaves its way through furniture design and ornamentation in these late Qing pieces, perhaps more than any other period of Chinese furniture. It's not frivolous. It's not silly; it's sometimes playful and sometimes ironic. We recently sold a pair of chairs, for example, with red seats and black structural members. On the legs and the back were repeated a *ruyi* symbol, something that looks like a scepter and is thought capable of granting wishes.

All of which sounds very earnest and sincere, but the chairs were both culturally correct and fanciful. You looked at them and knew that someone had fun making them.

Chinese furniture is full of auspicious signs – bats (the word for bats, *fu,* sounds like the word for happiness or blessing), fungus (*lingzhi*, thought to give long life), clouds (which give water and therefore life), fish (a symbol of plenty, particularly for male children), and the color red (the color of prosperity and a prominent feature of traditional Chinese weddings), among them. And while the Chinese take these signs seriously, they also recognize that their application in life can seem whimsical, and this reflection shows up in furniture design.

These symbols also speak to the illiteracy of most Chinese. They might not be able to read the character for *fu* (happiness), but they could recognize a picture of a bat, whose name sounded identical. These symbols presented an important visual language.

For Westerners, the appearance of this late Qing furniture could not be more auspicious. It represents an unparalleled opportunity to own pieces from a society whose craftsmen long ago mastered some of the most basic concepts of art and design – simplicity and complexity, straight line and curve. The furniture is beautiful, and Western decorators have found that it enhances and completes rooms with Western themes, from Biedermeir to Bau Haus, from American colonial to French Deco.

It is available in enormous quantity and variety from China and at prices that belie its heritage, the end product of 3,000 years of civilization. It costs far less than American and European antiques as well as the more traditional, classical furniture from China.

It came about as the result of change in Chinese society in the 18th and 19th centuries, the latter part of the Qing dynasty. Qing emperors, descendants of the Manchus who conquered China from the north in 1644, brought political stability and an associated burst of prosperity and consumerism to China. The Manchus overthrew the last Ming emperor and ended a dynasty (1368-1644) that had sparked a cultural renaissance followed by civil war and political disintegration – a familiar pattern in Chinese dynastic history.

When most people think of great Chinese furniture, they likely picture the classical styles of the Ming – simple, elegant, authoritative designs made of rich-grained hardwoods. Ornamentation was, by some accounts, considered vulgar in loftier circles and was therefore kept to a minimum. The presence was austere and imperial. It bespoke a superior civilization.

And with good reason. Classical furniture generally belonged to the ruling elite of China. If you wanted to get ahead in China, you had to pass a series of rigorous exams based on the teachings of Confucius. Passing these exams meant a job with the government. The system had been in place for centuries and created a large class of both scholars and literati bureaucrats who spread the emperor's will through China's vast geography. Becoming one of these bureaucrats was the ticket to wealth, often vast wealth, and extensive household possessions. One Ming government official, for example, listed more than 600 beds among his household possessions.

The Manchu conquerors who overthrew the last Ming emperor in 1644 kept this exam system in place, but they also, unintentionally, expanded the notion of who could own luxury goods. They had arrived at the invitation of the last Ming emperor, who asked the armies of Manchuria to come to Beijing and help him put down a civil war. They came, they saw, they conquered, and they stayed, becoming the latest in a series of non-Chinese rulers of China.

The stability of their Qing dynasty combined with expanding trade and contacts with the West to create a vigorous economic expansion that spread beyond the ruling elite. A new and prosperous merchant class grew up, and these new rich built big mansions and ordered big furniture to fill it. The rise of a merchant class was a new phenomenon in China, although one that might not seem out of the ordinary to Western readers. Merchants, in Chinese society, occupied the bottom rung of the status ladder. The ruling elite settled comfortably at the top followed by peasants and artisans, then the lowly merchant.

And they were either not as knowledgeable about classical designs or not as interested, because their furniture was often more creative, more colorful, and more ornamental than that of the Ming.

Also, unlike classical Ming pieces, it is available. Westerner collectors developed a taste for classical Ming furniture almost from the moment they arrived China in force in the 18th century. And they collected it to oblivion.

Virtually all the Ming furniture is either in museums or private collections, and if you want to buy some, you generally have to visit the auction houses of Christie's and Sotheby's, and you generally have to bring along a sizeable bank account. A pair of Ming chairs might easily run $50,000.

The opposite holds true for late Qing pieces. Museums own bits of it. Private collectors own more, but the bulk is still in China, either in homes or government warehouses, and its owners are eager to sell. Average incomes in China have been on the rise since 1979, but in the late 1990s they still scarcely tipped the scales above $600 a year. Selling a few sticks of furniture could bring an extra year's wage.

This furniture also, sadly, represents the end of a cultural era. Elegant furniture making has been a well-honed craft and prolific industry in China for over a thousand years. And the tradition has been continuous. It weakened considerably with the political instability that followed the overthrow of the Qing dynasty in 1911, and splintered with the turmoil that came with the Japanese invasion in 1931, followed by World War II, civil war, and Communist rule.

The latter ejected any outward signs of a class society. It also, in the 1950s, brought starvation on a mass level, killing millions of Chinese. So it's not difficult to understand why the craft of fine furniture making became superfluous. And while China grew more prosperous in the 1980s and 1990s, it is still a poor country governed by an authoritarian state, and cabinet making has seen little or no revival. It may be gone forever.

On the trail of Chinese furniture, especially from the late Qing, it's important to stay loose – be flexible and willing to shift your perspectives a few degrees. China is different, and cultural things that come from China shouldn't be viewed through Western-colored glasses. Chapter Two, on Provenance, delves into the subject more deeply, but, in brief, what is considered "real" and important Chinese furniture in some circles is not necessarily what is, in fact, real and important.

You might even take a note from the pages of Chinese scholars themselves. The elite – high government officials and scholars – have valued antiques for centuries. They especially liked furniture with a crackled lacquer finish, just as Westerners do. But their concept of what made an antique – gu – was different from ours. Age was not a determining factor. A successful antique might well have been made recently. Similarly, a 300 year-old piece of furniture might not make the grade. An antique was a piece of furniture that was "morally ennobling," according to one ancient treatise on the subject.

It's an idea that may not make the cultural voyage to Western shores in its entirety, but it merits at least a beach head – the idea of antique as art, something that provokes thought and discussion or that encourages the contemplation of beauty. The gu of late Qing furniture makes for an exciting and adventurous prospect, indeed.

Late Qing collections are new to the market, and they have arrived in the hands of dealers, decorators, and retail customers more quickly than those of major collectors and museums, so trends in fashion may overtake assumptions about authenticity.

We've noted, for example, that, in the West, assumptions about the best of Chinese classical furniture are based at least in part on Western assumptions about what *should* be the paragon of the genre. Western collectors and museums have impressive collections of Ming furniture made from huanghuali wood with a clear, natural finish. However, such pieces have become the most sought after, and most expensive, at least in part because they became popular among Westerners living in Beijing in the 1930s and 1940s. The Chinese elite, through the early 17th century, by contrast, prized the much darker-colored zitan. When zitan grew scarce, craftsmen often dyed huanghuali – which was a much lighter brown – to match its color. When Westerners decided that the natural huanghuali was preferable, Chinese dealers often stripped off the dark dyes to suit their taste. In other words, what became the important and preferred finish on Chinese furniture may have depended more on Western preference than Chinese culture.

The same holds true for the pieces themselves. For decades, Western collectors have ignored furniture made of softwoods. Yet, while the written record on what the Chinese preferred is scant, what there is indicates a preference for softwoods.

All of which is by way of saying, "Buy it because you like it," not because of preconceived and possibly inaccurate notions about what's important. The record is still being written on furniture from the late Qing, and what's valuable to an individual depends in large part on individual taste. The craftsmanship in a piece – sophistication of design, quality of construction, intricacy of decoration – should be readily apparent to anyone who engages in even a quick perusal of this book. Beyond that, be adventurous. Expand your ideas about what works in home décor (banish the phrase, "My grandmother had a Chinese cabinet, and I didn't like it.") and try a small, delicate, altar table in the foyer or a food basket next to the living room couch. Antiques from the late Qing dynasty present an opportunity that may never pass this way again.

CHAPTER TWO:
PROVENANCE
From Chairs to Chairman Mao —Where Does It Come From?

Who/what/when/where/why? – it sounds like the opening line in your Journalism 101 class in college, but it's also one of the traditional keys to value for antique furniture ... Western antiques, that is. Not so for furniture from the Middle Kingdom. Remember, China's culture has been marching to the beat of its own drum for 3000 years, and in the 1950s and 1960s, its encounter with Mao Zedong added a truly bizarre and tragic twist.

The five "W's" describe provenance – the life story of a particular piece: who made it, where it was made, who bought it, who has owned it, where did it live most recently? Find me a chair made in the late 1700s in Boston and I might write you a check for six figures. Show me a chair made (and signed) by the maker in Boston in 1768, most recently part of the estate of Nelson Rockefeller, and I'll show you a ticket to early retirement in your new beach house in Palm Beach. Provenance isn't everything, but it covers items one through five on the top-10 list of things that will take you to antiques heaven.

But, as with most other things from the Middle Kingdom of China, you have to adjust your ideas about provenance when dealing with its antiques. The "what" and the "why" are obvious. A chair is what it looks like, and the why – while a bit more complex – is equally obvious. From there, things get problematic.

Furniture makers, for example, usually did not sign their pieces. Chinese culture was, and largely still is, immune from the Western inclination to glorify the individual – unless that individual happens to be the Son of Heaven himself, the emperor – so the idea of elevating a mere craftsman to notable status would have seemed alien. The Chinese equivalents of John Townsend certainly plied their trade and transformed rough planks of southern elm into elegant, enticing tables and chairs, and they were probably famous in their time and sought after by wealthy clients .... but we don't know who they were.

The buyer, not the maker, would have been the most likely candidate to have his chop (a stamp with a unique configuration of the owner's name, something similar to a signature) affixed to the piece, since he was the one with all the money and importance. And, in fact, some of the more exquisite smaller items, such as baskets, have the name of the owner and his address painted on them. The owner was sometimes responsible for the design itself. Furniture was frequently crafted at the home of the buyer, with close supervision and oral instructions on design.

But even the owner's name on furniture or accessories represent the exception (and it is sometimes applied in the restoration process). Furniture certainly signaled rank and status in Chinese society, but not as much as in Western circles. The few surviving, written descriptions of valuable items in a household, from both Ming and Qing dynasties, rarely pay much attention to furniture. And historical records have yielded few furniture inventory lists for specific Chinese households. The best known is that of a Ming government official, Yan Song, who was disgraced and had his furniture seized by the emperor (the furniture list included more than

This leather trunk has a company's chop in the form of a seal.

Detail of company's chop.

600 beds), but that list is unique. So we have no primary source that directly tells us what the furniture holdings might have looked like for households up and down the income scale.

So the "who" comes up missing in the search for provenance. "Where" and "when" offer a bit more help, but not much.

We can generally look at a table or cabinet and identify regional characteristics. A wardrobe made in Shaanxi province, home of the ancient capital Xian (and the tomb of the Emperor Qin, with its famous terra cotta warriors), usually has a more substantial presence – thicker wood, heavier legs, more authority – than one made in Ningbo, on the coast just south of Shanghai. In fact, some Chinese people say that residents of the coastal cities and towns were more superficial than those of Shaanxi, and the furniture design reflects that.

The craftsmen of Suzhou (Shaanxi and Suzhou were two of the premier furniture-making regions in China) were considered especially adept at bamboo tables and chairs, and those in the southern province of Canton were often considered the best at intricately painted decorations on lacquered furniture. But while such statements are informed and helpful, they are not necessarily definitive. A Shaanxi-style cabinet could have been made in Shanxi, just to north, or in Suzhou, near Shanghai, or even way down south in Canton. Important furniture was made throughout the south and central regions of China. Without a signature, it's impossible to know the exact origin of a piece.

"When" trips over similar stumbling blocks. Specific periods can tend towards certain styles. During the 18th century, for example, pieces with red or black lacquered coloring generally had a thicker coat of lacquer than similar pieces from the 19th century. Over time, that thickness produces a "crackling" effect in the finish, called *duanwen* – prized now by Westerners and for centuries by the Chinese. The thicker lacquer also bubbles and chips more than thinner coats. (On cabinets, the latter usually occurs around the edge of doors and door openings, as well as at corners. The same process often occurs on legs as well, since, in

13

recent years, cabinets may have been stored on cement floors.)

Similarly, more intricate painting and carving might indicate that a piece was made before the mid-1800s.

But, again, this is not definitive. A thickly lacquered piece from the 19th century might be unusual, but it is not rare. It's true that certain elements of style allow for general dating. The presence of westerners living in Beijing during the late 1800s, for example, brought the influence of Western, often Victorian, furniture design.

Bamboo shelves or tables often developed a less delicate, more solid appearance under Western influence. Cupboards sometimes acquired glass doors in deference to the Western notion of using cupboards for display. The Chinese idea was to use cupboards to hide things away and secure them.

But stylistically, these same pieces could have come from the turn of the century or even the early 20th century. Some details of style as well as finish and construction techniques might help narrow the time frame, but it's difficult to come up with more than a general sense of period.

So, while certain elements of style can allow an antique dealer to say that a piece is likely to be from the late 18th century, a more accurate characterization might be a range, i.e. late 18th to early 19th century. This could be construed as splitting hairs, however, and sincere, knowledgable dealers will often say a piece dates from the 1880s, 1820s, 1850s, etc., code for the late 19th, early 19th, or mid-19th century.

Chinese furniture design evolved slowly, slowly. A table that dates from the 12th century is not terribly different in design from those we see from the 18th and 19th centuries. So if a dealer tells you a piece was made in specific year, say 1762, that dealer is likely uninformed or ill-intentioned.

So we've eliminated three fifths of what goes into provenance. And keep in mind that the vague presence of these three "Ws" doesn't just apply to vernacular furniture. It's as true of the authoritative collections of Ming hardwood furniture at Boston's Museum of Fine Arts and New York's Metropolitan Museum of Art as it is of the wedding cabinet on the floor at an antique dealer in Ohio.

Tracing the thread of provenance became even more tangled when the culture clashed with Chairman Mao, and lost.

Mao and his Communist cadres eliminated much of traditional Chinese culture and rearranged the rest. The making and owning of luxury furniture was – understandably – not spared the turmoil.

During the Cultural Revolution of the 1960s, brigades of young Communists, Red Guards, attempted to rout out remaining vestiges of China's "olds," the class society that had dominated and oppressed ordinary Chinese for centuries.

Their zeal marked a change of heart on Mao's part. During much of the 1950s, Mao seemed to accept that while the concept of a classless society was revolutionary, adaptation to it would be more evolutionary. His patience vanished in mid-1960s, and the overnight goal became zero tolerance for class-consciousness and its trappings.

Red Guards rampaged through cities, villages, and homes – destroying or seizing art objects and furniture, and often the people who owned it. The furniture was sometimes burned in the village streets (often, after the Red Guards left, residents might rush out of their homes and pull furniture from the fire. The remaining burn marks can sometimes be seen on pieces that survived.).

But the Red Guards carted much of it off to giant warehouses, "owned" by the Peoples Liberation Army (PLA), where it sat for the better part of a decade.

After Mao passed and reformer Deng Xiaoping rose to power, government officials in the early 1980s apparently concluded that by imprisoning the furniture – bourgeois roots notwithstanding – they were punishing the masses, who could actually make use of it.

So much of it was redistributed, with no thought to its original owners. A farmer in a remote village in Xinjiang, near the northern border, might receive a table once owned by a scholar in Canton and intended for painting delicate landscapes on silk scrolls. Not too surprisingly, that farmer would have been more likely to use the table for butchering chickens or repairing farm implements than for the artistic exploration of Taoist concepts of man and nature.

Such "provenance" described the fate of a significant portion of the Chinese furniture that now finds its way to Western shores. It was given to rural households in China where it received use considerably rougher than its noble origins. It might have been left in the sun and rain, or shared quarters with farm animals. One collector refers to "ten thousand years of wear in a few moments."

Since late Qing furniture was "discovered" by Western collectors in the 1990s, its owners have generally been delighted to sell. For the decade of the 1990s, the average annual income in China was about $600, so selling a few sticks of furniture could have a much greater impact than using them. But these pieces were, and are, often in terrible condition – broken, worn, discolored, modified. Some of them are refinished and repaired in China, in the workshops in the south, near the distribution points of Macau and Hong Kong, or around Shanghai. Some arrives in the U.S. and, to a lesser extent Europe, in "as is" condition. But the rustic appearance belies its original use and what little we know of the provenance. The most recent Chinese owners rarely had any connection with its original owners.

Pieces awaiting repair in a southern Chinese warehouse.

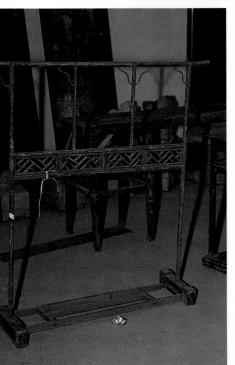

There's more to this bizarre story. Not all the furniture was redistributed out of the PLA warehouses. Much of it apparently stayed put until the army needed to raise money – either for individual commanders or to help finance the PLA itself. The PLA was, and is, a self-financing organization. It owns factories and even entire industries so that its budget can remain independent of the country's economic well-being. It appears that antiques marched to the same beat.

We hear from various sources in China of vast warehouses organized by categories – large painted cabinets in one, bamboo furniture in another, tables in another, chairs in another, etc. – which the PLA periodically put up for sale, flooding the market with a particular type of furniture.

The last three years have brought an abundance of bamboo furniture, courtesy of the PLA, for example. And antique shoppers on the streets of Macau and Shanghai in the summer of 1999 might have marveled that so many shops suddenly carried large stacking cabinets. There was even a virtual parade of processional chariots when we visited Macau in October 1999. Chinese antique dealers don't like to talk about PLA warehouses full of furniture because they know it doesn't appeal to the romantic notions that Westerners sometimes attach to antiques. But they are a fact of the business.

We're told that when these warehouses go on the block, the antique dealers – Western and Chinese – who have the best connections and know how to spend money in the most productive ways get first choice. And vast arrays of the best of these pieces will probably remain tucked away, part of some general's retirement plan, until prices soar in five to 10 years.

There's nothing wrong with this process. In fact, it means that many of the better pieces of Chinese furniture were saved the indignity of the farmyard or, worse, the bonfire. The PLA storage facilities probably lacked anything approaching temperature control, and wood furniture stored on cement floors may explain why the colored lacquer on cabinet legs has chipped away.

But the entire process adds an interesting dimension for Western enthusiasts attempting to apply the concepts of provenance to Chinese antiques. It just doesn't work. The idea of family furniture heirlooms cherished from generation to generation, then sold at an estate sale, is nonexistent. It is possible for Westerners to travel the villages of China and buy old furniture that belongs to descendents of its original owners, but such occasion is rare and such furniture is usually rustic, not fine.

The real chain of ownership starts with the original owners, moves to the state, then either directly to new Chinese owners and then to antiques dealers, or else directly from the state to antiques dealers. The whole process has a decidedly institutional stamp.

But remember this is China, a country dominated by institutional self interest and institutional inertia. The Chinese don't operate the way Westerners do. They bring vastly different traditions and motives to similar situations. The dynamic is different, just as it was in the 18th century, when a British envoy to China was told by the emperor that Western inventions, to say nothing of attitudes, were of little use in China.

But keep in mind that this process, while lacking in romance, creates tremendous opportunity for Western buyers. Most Chinese antique dealers really aren't connoisseurs as much as they are traders – buy low, sell a little bit higher. So antiques are priced as much by availability as by market value. And since these pieces often flood onto the market by category, their availability is usually ready, and their price is low.

So at the risk of sounding like a real estate broker, when you see a piece you like, "there has never been a better time to buy than now." That piece and its price probably represent a market dynamic – more supply than demand – which has kept the price low for a window of time. And that window will eventually shut.

Consider this: we recently sold an eight-foot long altar table made of walnut. It was made in the mid-to-late 18th century, was in flawless condition and drop-dead gorgeous. It went out the door for $5,000, on its way to the living room of a large estate in Virginia. An 18th century English or French walnut table in that condition would cost at least double.

Determining what a piece of old Chinese furniture should look like presents a dilemma and sometimes a controversy.

The key point to remember is that these antiques age well. The predominant wood in late Qing furniture is a Chinese elm, either southern or northern, and its deep colors and rich, lively grain grow more beautiful with time and wear. Other woods used in this furniture enjoy the same characteristics, and even the most weathered or abused piece has a rich, warm patina when cleaned up.

As with any antique furniture, the most valuable pieces are those in unrestored condition with the fewest blemishes. These pieces are available, but hard to find, and, as one might expect, expensive – although still less than comparable Western antiques.

But much of this furniture, as we discuss in the section on provenance, had a rough time, first at the hands of Mao's Red Guards and later under the stewardship of new owners. Farmers and peasants acquired many important pieces, and they put it to work in their daily lives, leaving it with gouges, cracks, breaks, and worn coloring – in short, leaving it in a condition not true to the culture that originally produced it. Some Western buyers prefer this condition. It fits nicely with the rustic look popular in some American homes, and the furniture often costs less than pieces that have been restored.

There is also cultural value in pieces that have been worn down and worn out. They tell an accurate story of changes in Chinese society. Westerners may or may not approve of Mao's China and its drive to scour traditional Chinese culture, but it happened, nonetheless, and battered cabinets, chairs, and tables show it.

But the end results may not reflect Western tastes nearly as well as it does Chinese history. The rustic look generally doesn't show up in the pages of Architectural Digest or the room settings of finely decorated homes. There is a lot of room between rustic and perfect, and that territory — restoration — makes up the biggest segment of the market. Its goal is decorative pieces that will make it in those settings.

There are several approaches – some aimed at restoring the furniture to its original condition, some designed to suggest a piece's original finish, and some designed to replace it.

The first approach – restoration to original – is quite difficult. The original finishes are like China itself, an onionskin of complexity that defies modern-day efforts at repetition. Pieces with a clear, natural wood finish are not so problematic, but those with either solid color or painted scenes can be patched or touched up only in a minor way. Any major effort at reproduction is time consuming, expensive, and often beyond the reach of modern day craftsmen.

Consider the technique that goes into a small red cabinet. Chinese craftsmen were masters of layering different colors to produce a desired tone and depth in the final finish. They might start with black, followed by dark red, followed by a lighter red, followed by a brighter red. In between the coats of color would be layers of shellac, varnish, and lots of hand rubbing to make the color seamless.

One of the favorite woods of China's rulers was *zitan*, a rich, dark wood that was extremely hard. The key word, here, is "was" because zitan was cut to extinction during the Ming dynasty. Furniture makers often tried to imitate its color on soft woods by layering red and black lacquer, creating a black that was deeper and warmer than it was intense and opaque. It's not an easy color to match, especially if the work is done outside of China.

So complete restoration becomes difficult, perhaps impossible on many pieces. Large swaths of color might have been worn down to the wood; some of the red or black in the final color may have been worn down to some of the more muted shades or colors of red. A red lacquered cabinet may show specs of the black that constitutes the initial layer of color.

Given the poor condition of most of the furniture, the goal becomes not restoration but a refinishing that preserves and enhances the existing patina.

And that patina can be gorgeous – worn colors, bare woods, mottled appearances, these are what has made furniture from the late Qing dynasty so exciting. If treated well in the refinishing process, they become lively and warm additions to a room filled with Western décor, old or new.

Even then, the refinishing process can be controversial in some circles. Different buyers obviously have different ideas about what looks beautiful in their homes, and antiques dealers in China try to adapt their restorations with different customers in mind, sometimes altering the appearance of a piece entirely to satisfy a particular market. In a very general way, the Western market for Chinese pieces breaks down into two segments – European and American.

Furniture refinished for European buyers – especially on the continent – often has a high gloss. It's the way they like it, and it can be quite beautiful. If done correctly the finish requires a multistep process that uses traditional Chinese lacquer (made from the sap of the lacquer tree) and shellac, another natural product. The correct number of coats, the requisite amount of rubbing and sanding between coats, is a fantastically difficult and sometimes proprietary process, handed down among generations of furniture makers, and it produces a finish that brings out the patina of the wood and protects it from water, wear, and fading.

Sometimes what's left of the original color will be stripped off completely and the bare wood given a glossy finish of either shellac or lacquer. And sometimes the color remnants are left, producing a finish with mottled coloring and beautiful texture.

This high-gloss finish has lately found an enthusiastic market in America because it creates furniture that blends well in elegant settings. The gloss also underscores the line and shape of the piece itself. It has, however, also generated controversy because the gloss, to some, creates an appearance of "new."

But remember, appreciating Chinese antiques often requires a new set of filters, a change in perspectives. Are we looking at Chinese furniture through Western perceptions of the way it should be? As nearly as we can tell, no one really knows how the furniture was originally finished. And in all likelihood, it was not finished to follow a single group of guidelines. Different regions and different craftsmen made furniture in different styles. And different owners gave their own instructions for design. This may be especially true of the late Qing dynasty, when an increasingly wealthy merchant class broke away from some of the more rigid traditions in furniture making.

If the Chinese wrote " how to" descriptions or manuals for the finishing process during the late Qing years, they haven't survived. In fact, there is only one surviving manual for Chinese furniture making, and it predates the Qing by centuries. Even it is by no means comprehensive, and judging by furniture produced at the same time, its rules were not followed with any great degree of loyalty.

And Western descriptions of Chinese furniture have focused almost entirely on the clear finishes of hardwood pieces from the late Ming and early Qing years. There is precious little written about softwood furniture.

However, the clear lacquer and shellac were readily available to 18th and 19th century furniture makers, and the skill needed to achieve a glossy look is not modern. It is old, must be learned, and takes tremendous time.

So it seems reasonable to assume that a highly lacquered gloss may have originally been a question of preference – popular in some Chinese households and not in others. Whether it's any more genuine than a thin coat of clear lacquer, shellac, or even a wax as the final finish is difficult to state with a degree of certainty.

And in some contexts, it just doesn't matter. We know a French dealer who sells late Qing furniture, and she has half the refinishing – including a complete strip down of the color – done in China, then ships the pieces to France for a French polish. The result is a gorgeous, deep, uniform finish that does justice to the design of the cabinets, tables, and chairs.

Similarly, the beautiful Chinese red that graces so much of this furniture has rarely survived the decades in tact. Often applied in different hued layers, it gets worn down to different layers, often to the bare wood, for a richly varied appearance. Clear lacquer can dress it up and preserve it.

We sell some pieces with a high gloss finish and have placed them in apartments on the Upper East Side of New York city, Greenwich, Connecticut, and the north shore of Chicago as well as in homes across the economic spectrum. Clients love them because they can be parked next to a Chippendale high boy and look right at home.

We also sell pieces that have a less "finished" appearance – with either a thin coat of clear lacquer or wax as the final finish. The mottled, textured appearances remain and keep the pieces interesting, but the patina is closer to the surface, more immediate, less shiny. A piece with this finish would feel just as comfortable next to the Chippendale high boy, but the finishes would compliment each other by contrast rather than similarity.

A word, here, about finishes we find uninteresting and which detract from value and appearance. Some restoration shops strip away all color, often in imitation of that elusive standard, the clear, hardwood finishes of the classical furniture that has mistakenly become associated with the pinnacle of Chinese furniture making. Never mind that they're working with softwoods and that they are obliterating the intent of the furniture maker and his patron. These shops work from a faulty perception of what is important.

So a red wedding cabinet becomes a natural-wood wedding cabinet. A painted, tapered cabinet dons a natural wood finish, etc. Altar tables that were loving and playfully colored a famous Chinese red become and dull, non-Chinese brown. If this is your taste, that's fine. But to us, the process takes the furniture even farther from its original condition and eliminates the patina that is beautiful, hard-earned and unique to Chinese furniture.

Other restoration shops strip away what's left of the original color and replace it with new color. It happens frequently with red wedding cabinets. Remember what we said about the complexity with which color was applied by the original Chinese craftsmen – multiple layers, multiple rubbing, multiple colors. It produced a seamless layer and great depth of final color. The new craftsmen don't even try to imitate that complexity and skill. They rub on one or two coats of color and call it a day.

And the results show it. The color looks skin deep and the brush and rubbing marks are readily apparent. The patina is destroyed. The *gu* is gone.

Another flaw to look for is in the clear lacquer that often becomes a final coat. The Chinese lacquer is wonderful stuff for its ability to both preserve and enhance. It protects wood and paint from aging and water, while it brings out the patina. However, as we've noted, the skill required applying it is difficult and, in a cliché of modern times, not one readily learned by impatient, young Chinese craftsmen and women.

They often rush the job. When considering a purchase, you should look for evidence of their impatience – streaks and drips in the lacquer, both on the exterior finishes and on the interior wood. The inside of a door jamb, for example, might show drips of lacquer that ran off from the exterior. If applied well, the lacquer is not only invisible, but draws out and emboldens the color of the paint underneath. Applied quickly and poorly, it is apparent and often dulls the underlying colors.

That doesn't necessarily mean that a piece is not worth buying. Our philosophy is that if it speaks to you, buy it. Case in point: we recently had in our inventory two pairs of bamboo, yoke back chairs. Their shape was stunning, unlike any we have ever seen, and they were comfortable as well. But the final coat of clear lacquer was apparent, on close inspection, on the wooden seats. We bought them anyway because they were still beautiful – a telling comment on the Chinese sense of design – but priced them lower than we normally would have. If you see lacquer streaks in a number of pieces in a dealer's collection, that should give you some hint about the quality of the inventory.

CHAPTER FOUR:
FAKES
The Real vs. the Somewhat Real

The Chinese, as everyone knows, excel at the art of reproduction. They have been practicing this art probably for as long as they have been making originals.

Even in the 18th century, when trade with Europe was expanding and Western goods were all the rage among Chinese consumers, craftsmen who lived in the coastal regions would makes copies of the European goods and ship them to the interior provinces to be sold as the real thing. One hundred years ago, Chinese forgers were making copies of Chinese artifacts that were made one thousand years ago.

Sometimes, copies and forgeries, as in the above examples, are an effort to deceive, but sometimes they are an effort to compliment and preserve. This is one of those cultural distinctions we've noted elsewhere in the book, and it may have little importance for antique buyers, but it's worth a sentence or two.

The idea is that if something is beautiful once, it can be beautiful twice if an exact copy is made. Consider the process as something of a compliment to the art and design of the original as well as the product of a society that has, for centuries, placed little value on the status of the individual, on being unique. Chinese culture has also tended to view time cyclically. The calendar started over with each new emperor so the concept of assigning a higher value to one thing because it is chronologically older than something else is a bit off the track in China. And don't forget that the Chinese word for antique, *gu* (Chapter One), doesn't mean "older" so much as it means "better." There are old antiques and new antiques.

That said, a lot of fakes have nothing to do with a cyclical view of the calendar. They are nothing more than an effort to deceive, and antique buyers should know how to spot the deception. It's usually not that hard.

And, fortunately, with decorative pieces from the late Qing dynasty, it's not that common. You're far more likely to find reproductions or pieces that have been substantially reconstructed with new wood than you are to find outright fakes.

Let's start with the use of new wood to patch up old furniture. It's not at all unusual, in both Western and Asian circles, to use new wood to make minor patches on an old piece (and then there is the sign we saw outside a shop in Bali – "Antiques made to order."). The antique value becomes less on any such piece. It happens in order to make the piece pre-

sentable and saleable. But at some point the piece stops being old.

We once visited a furniture shop in China and saw a bookshelf undergoing an unusual restoration routine. The piece had five shelves and open sides, back, and front, supported by vertical posts on each corner. But the only piece of old, original wood left was one of the shelves. Everything else – four shelves and four corner posts – was fresh off the truck from whatever passes for Home Depot in China. We have similarly seen cabinets where one entire side is new wood and tables with one, two, or three legs replaced. Remember that most of this furniture sustained significant damage, both through neglect and breakage. The question becomes how much restoration you want in the piece you are buying.

The best way to guard against aberrations in authenticity is by picking a good dealer. Find someone who can speak authoritatively about the background of pieces, where they come from, what they were used for, the approximate period in which they were made, and the history of the period itself. A dealer who cares enough to learn about the culture that produced these pieces will likely care enough to make sure the quality is high.

More specifically, ask whether any part of the piece you're interested in has new construction. You can look for yourself, and we'll show you how in a paragraph or two, but qualifying your dealer is an important part of the process.

We go through the same process when we buy furniture in China. We not only scrutinize each piece but also scrutinize the dealer who's selling it. We've found antique dealers in China to be about as honest and truthful as antique dealers in the U.S. It varies. If he or she insists that a piece is all original with original finish and hardware but we can spot some restoration work, that dealer loses a lot of credibility and probably a lot of business. More importantly, we rarely buy a piece that we have not seen and photographed in its unrestored condition, so we can see what was broken and what was eventually fixed or replaced. And if we haven't been able to do that, we insist on being given a photograph of the piece in its original condition. We then show these photographs to our U.S. customers who are considering a purchase.

If your dealer doesn't have an original-condition photograph and doesn't know as much as you had hoped for about the piece, but you're in love with it nonetheless, snoop around a bit yourself. If it's a cabinet, open the doors and spend some time with your head inside. Do the structural pieces look like they were cut with hand tools or do they have the neat, crisp edges that come from a modern power saw? What about the inside of the side and back panels; do they look weathered and old or freshly made? Try to find places where the wood has contracted and exposed the edge of one piece of wood where it used to join another piece. Sometimes you can see the bare, raw wood, and if it looks bright and yellow or white, it's probably new wood.

Look at the back of the cabinet for the same signs – weathered-looking wood and rough cuts instead of clean ones. If possible, try to look at the bottom of the cabinet's legs. They should look as if they've been dragged around a bit, even chipped away at the edges. If they're squared off, neat, and even, that's one sign of a new leg. The bottom of legs is also a spot that doesn't get lacquered or colored, so you can often gauge the relative age of the wood.

The same process works for tables and chairs. Look underneath or turn them upside down, always checking for signs of weathered wood and cuts made by imprecise hand tools. The Chinese sometimes moved chairs by dragging them across the floor on the backs of their rear legs. So some wear and chipping in those spots might be expected, although restoration craftsmen sometimes just cut the legs down to remove excessive damage to the bottoms.

The latter practice raises an interesting point about alteration and repair. It's not unusual to find tables that have been shortened or one piece of furniture that has been pieced together from others. Such pieces can often be authentic and culturally accurate. The Chinese sometimes did this for themselves, to make a piece more useful, but more often they did it in the late 19th and early 20th centuries to accommodate Western buyers living in China.

We've seen Eight Immortals tables, which normally stand about 34 inches tall, cut down to become coffee table height. Such alterations are not necessarily a reason to shy away. The Victoria and Albert Museum in London owns one of the preeminent Chinese furniture collections in the world, and it includes just such an altered piece, as does the National Museum in Taipei.

Again – buy what you like, the pieces that speak to you, but know what you are buying.

Sometimes, however, you can't know what you're buying. The work is just too good, the fakery too clever. We've talked in this chapter about looking for new wood in old pieces. But we know of dealers in China who use old wood to rebuild old pieces. We've seen hundreds of beams and timbers taken from old houses that were torn down. Their faded lumber was stacked in the yard of one production shop. The wood is truly old, and it goes into rebuilding and repairing battered old furniture, which then sells for high prices because of its original condition. Some of it may even go into making entirely new pieces, although that level of forgery occurs largely at the high end of the scale, the collector and museum quality pieces that came from the wealthiest, most elite Chinese homes and which command the highest prices.

For those not in that league, it's extremely important to know why you are buying a piece of antique furniture. It's easy to get caught up in the "investment value" of a piece when that issue is not necessarily the most relevant. If you're buying antique furniture as an investment, you should load up on research and become as knowledgeable as a dealer.

Even so, while antiques were rated one of the best investments of the 1980s, they were also one of the least liquid. A Chippendale high boy may be worth more this year than last, but selling it at the higher price is tricky. It has to appreciate beyond a dealer markup before it can return a profit to the retail buyer. Investing in antiques is a lot like investing in art. Buy it because you like it and because it will bring you great pleasure when you look at it. Even in ancient China, "examining one's antiques" was considered an appropriate pastime for scholars and gentlemen. But to buy a piece because you plan to resell it at a higher price requires great skill and great patience.

CHAPTER FIVE

THE PIECES
Furniture and Accessories

LARGE CABINETS

Westerners might call them armoires or wardrobes, but the large Chinese cabinet showed more versatility than a mere closet replacement. It was used to store clothing and bedding but also just about anything the master or mistress of a household wanted to keep secure and out of sight. Precious objects such as a porcelain vase or root wood brush pot or a rolled-up painting might be stored in a cabinet when not on display or being used. Western buyers have kept pace with Chinese notion of versatility by using cabinets as entertainment centers. (Those early craftsmen showed great foresight in designing furniture to accommodate the large-screen TV.)

Big cabinets come in two broad categories – tapered, usually with a removable center post between the doors, and rectangular. Hinges can be brass (rarely original) or wooden, carved in the shape of a lotus blossom or, occasionally, an acorn or some other object from nature. Wooden hinges allow the doors to be removed easily, which gave the Chinese easy access for storing large objects or laying clothes lengthwise – and which gives Westerners easy access for stereo systems and TVs. We have one client who bought a large tapered cabinet with a removable center post, and she keeps her 32-inch TV in it. When it comes time to watch the tube, she pops the post out. The process takes about 2 seconds and gives her a television cabinet that looks infinitely better than a modern-day entertainment center.

One of the most popular varieties is the wedding cabinet – generally about 72 inches tall, 42 inches wide and 24 inches deep and painted red (the color of good luck and prosperity). A wedding cabinet was often the centerpiece of a bride's dowry. They are beautiful, with a large, round brass plate – sometimes with carving etched into the perimeter – in the middle of the doors, and liven up a room. We have one that doubles as a bookshelf in our office. We keep the doors open, and it creates a warm presence as well as a practical work space.

A wedding cabinet works best as a decorator's piece. For collectors, they have dubious value. They are ubiquitous among Western dealers, and they are very difficult to date. They look much the same whether made in the 20th or 19th century. Some, such as the one pictured here with its carved header, have detail that suggests some age, but such detail is no guarantee. Wedding cabinets are perhaps the most susceptible among Chinese furniture to alteration and refinishing, and it's not at all unlikely to find a wedding cabinet with an old detail and everything else new.

Beautiful red wedding
cabinet with carved header.

They are frequently rearranged to accommodate entertainment centers. The traditional drawer and shelf combination that usually stretches across the middle of the interior is often lowered to the bottom to hold a TV. You will occasionally find a black wedding cabinet whose color is original – but when you find one painted green or yellow, it's color is new.

Finishes range from a natural wood to burgundy to purple to solid red or black – sometimes with painted scenes on the doors. The subject matter of those scenes offers clues about use within a Chinese household. Pictures of women or children (always males) usually suggest a wife's or concubine's quarters. More philosophical settings, such as a landscape of mountains and streams, might belong in a scholar's studio.

Other cabinet types include stacking cabinets (with a separate upper piece to store hats or seasonal cloth-

Above & Right: Small cabinets like these serve well as bedside cabinets.

Left: Example of a large medicine/herb cabinet from the mid-1800s.

ing), and, one of our favorites, the medicine cabinet – *bai yan chu*, or hundred eye cabinet. Chinese doctors labeled each of the multitude of drawers with the names of herbs and medicines (various mushrooms, reindeer antlers, etc.) to fix what ails you.

Other cabinet sizes: You name, they made it. We've had cabinets as small as eight inches high – delightful miniatures of the bigger ones – and as tall as 13 feet. They come low to the ground, double-sided, delicately tapered to about 48 inches tall, and even cube-shaped at 18 inches on each side. We sometimes sell small, tapered, red cabinets that stand about 24 inches tall and 18 inches wide

Customers use Chinese cabinets for dining room sideboards, living room stereo storage, bookshelves, bedside tables, and kitchen cupboards. There is actually a traditional Chinese kitchen cabinet, designed to circulate air around fruits and vegetables without letting in light. The lower compartments housed live chickens and other fowl, destined for dinner.

The Chinese made cabinets in such variety because they were the primary storage facilities within a household. Closets are a Western invention, still a rarity in Chinese societies from Hong Kong to Taipei to Beijing, and drawers never received widespread usage. You won't find a chest of drawers or dresser in the Chinese vocabulary … and with good reason. Drawers are harder to lock.

Cabinets, however, could successfully keep valuables away from prying eyes and sticky fingers.

A wealthy Chinese household put a roof over lots of heads – servants, concubines, and relatives. The ideal home was thought to have five generations living under one roof. And since it was considered a great insult to put a lock on the door to a room (the bitterest divisions within a family would result in doors being nailed shut), cabinets and trunks and boxes, most of which could be locked, allowed for secure storage.

Red lacquer kitchen cabinet.

TRUNKS:

Trunks fulfill much the same storage function as cabinets in a Chinese household, and, like cabinets, they come in a huge variety of sizes – some as big as a bed, others as tiny as a matchbox. The larger sizes were used primarily for seasonal clothes and bedding while smaller sizes held items ranging from hair ornaments to important documents.

Among the most popular among Western aficionados are leather trunks, ranging in size from a small suitcase to a large footlocker. They can be made out of wood with a painted exterior or out of leather – pigskin, actually – stretched over a thin wooden frame. The latter are sometimes finished with a clear coat of lacquer, which protects the leather and enhances the patina. Westerners sometimes use them for coffee tables (mounted on a low, wooden stand) or just something decorative for the floor or atop a cabinet.

Black wooden trunk with gilt design on stand.

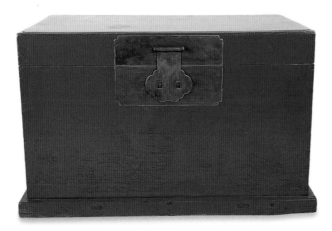

Red wooden trunk with base.

Red leather trunk with rounded lid
and an embossed and gilt design.

24

KANG TABLES
- Cold winds … warm furniture

The arrival of winter in China brings a cold shift in wind direction, one whose eventual result is some of the furniture that makes its way across the Pacific and into Western living rooms.

Instead of hot, humid summer air flowing up from the South China Sea, winter brings cold winds down from Siberia, plunging temperatures in northern and central China well below freezing. But the Chinese, masters of form and function, designed their homes and furniture to keep them warm.

One or several rooms in a Chinese home usually included a *kang,* a large platform built of bricks or packed earth. In the center of the kang was either a fire pit or stove flue, kept burning day and night to keep the kang warm.

Most of the day's activities – eating, working, sleeping, painting, reading, talking with friends, even cooking – took place on the kang, and furniture was specifically designed to accommodate it. Kang tables, cupboards, and cabinets were short and designed to be lifted up from the floor onto the kang and used while reclining or sitting with your legs over the edge of the kang.

But what started as a way to keep warm in China translates into elegant designs for Western homes. Kang tables are 18 to 21 inches high, perfect as coffee tables, end tables, or any place where a low table enhances design. Kang tables often come 30 to 36 inches square, but they can also be rectangular and with exterior table top dimensions as small 12 inches.

Red lacquer kang table with 3 drawers.

TABLES AND CHAIRS

Imagine yourself the dinner guest of a wealthy Chinese trader in the city Chengdu, Sichuan province. From the street, you approach the front gate of a massively walled mansion and are ushered inside. You see several buildings and multiple courtyards, all separate homes for different members of the family, but the main hall is an obvious structure, rising on a grand scale before you. Inside this great reception hall, you see a scene fairly typical of Chinese homes on any scale – on the north wall, opposite the entrance, sits a shrine to the ancestors, the core of religious worship in most of China. And in front of that shrine you would almost certainly find an altar table – arguably the most important piece of furniture in a Chinese home.

The standard word for table is *an* and perhaps the most common type of altar table is the *qiaotou an* – the raised end table. Long and thin with upturned ends, the altar table, when placed in front of a shrine, might hold incense or an offering of fruit, flowers, or food – an attempt to encourage the goodwill of the ghosts of ancestors when they visit the family home.

Elmwood altar table with everted ends and carved spandrels.

The altar table makes an important point about Chinese homes, because the table was not important for what it was so much as where it was. The home played a critical role in Chinese society because it was the vessel that contained the family, the basic unit of survival and prosperity. Three of the five relationships that form the core of Confucianism relate to families – husband and son, husband and wife, elder brother and younger brother. Homes were the center of life– birth, marriage, funerals, religious worship, artistic endeavor, and education – and their focus was inward. The face they showed to the outside world was usually a massive, forbidding wall. Architectural personality was saved for those inside.

The point here is that furniture was only important within the context of the home. Indeed, the Chinese word for furniture, *jiaju*, literally means "implements of the house," tools used within a living environment. So the altar table became important because of where it was placed in the home. Remove it from the setting, and its importance changes.

The term "altar table," in fact, is probably a Western invention. They were used throughout a Chinese home for aesthetic purposes, set up against a wall, perhaps to display vases, sculptures, flowers, and *objets d'art*. Common sizes range from 36 inches to 8 feet long, 14 to 20 inches wide, and 33 to 36 inches tall.

The style of these fabulous tables – designed entirely to display beautiful objects – covers a wide range. They might have horsehoof legs, *mati,* or straight legs or solid vertical panels, recessed waist or straight waist or beaded, and a floating panel (made to contract and expand with temperature changes) for the tabletop or a single plank of wood. A flat altar table with no inverted ends, recessed waist, and horsehoof legs is commonly termed "Ming style."

But let's go back to the reception hall, the most important room in a Chinese home. Increasingly, in the Qing dynasty, you would have seen another table set in front of and up against the altar table. It would likely have been square and pulled out into the center of the room for eating or as a place to sit and converse with guests. More often than not, this table was a *ban xian zhuo,* an Eight Immortals table. It got its name from a play on words. The Eight Immortals belong in the Buddhist pantheon, and these tables were made to seat eight people, two to a side, on benches or stools.

(These benches were generally 36 to 40 inches long, about 8 inches deep and about 20 inches tall. The top might have been a solid piece of wood but just as likely it could have been made of cane. Benches served another function in this home, one similar to the altar table. Scholars used them in their studios for displaying precious objects.)

In more humble homes, the Eight Immortals table was even more versatile, serving as altar table, eating table, and kitchen table.

Back in our reception hall, you would not have seen furniture in the middle of the room – a Western concept – but you would probably have seen furniture against the wall, with windows overlooking a courtyard. There would likely have been pairs of chairs with a low table set between them. Chinese often favored groupings of threes, and as an honored guest in this house, you might have been invited to sit in one of these pairs of chairs for an intimate conversation. The table between you might have held some food or a vase with flowers. And it would have measured about 24 inches square and 18 inches tall, just about the correct size for an end table set next to a couch in a Western living room.

When tea arrived, the servants would have gone to another wall in the reception hall to pull out a tea table, standing about 33 inches tall and perhaps 16 inches long and nine inches wide. They invariably come in pairs, and our customers buy them as flower stands or hallways tables. They can be made of solid wood or bamboo.

The fact that you, a guest in the home, are seated in a chair at all indicates that you enjoy some status in the eyes of your host. Especially during the Ming dynasty, chairs were reserved for the most important people. Everyone else – including, often, the wife – was shown to the nearest stool.

The evolution of seating in China starts with reed mats about a thousand years ago, and works its way up low platforms, then to portable stools, thought to be an import from nomadic tribes to the north. Sometime in the Tang dynasty (AD 618-907), Chinese upper classes went from sitting on mats to elevating themselves onto stools and chairs. The first recorded use of a stool is a picture showing the emperor using it to mount a horse, and somewhere along the line it was adapted to seating. But the elevated seat, a physical symbol of elevated status, retained its high rank, and only the most important people were given chairs. Such exclusivity had no doubt eroded by the late Qing dynasty, but the chair

Eight Immortals table with carved spandrels, elmwood, ca. 1850. $2000-$4000.

was, nonetheless, considered an important place to be.

It was also considered a relatively warm place to be. Homes in the cold central and northern provinces generally had stone floors, which, obviously, became quite cold. So the Chinese often made their chairs high enough to keep the occupant's feet off the ground … which makes them a workable size for Westerners. One charming addition to the seating plan was the footstool, low (8 to 10 inches off the ground) wooden platforms that allow one to stretch the legs while avoiding the floor. Park one of these mini-ottomans in front of your favorite, overstuffed living room chair, and you will wonder why Ethan Allan never came up with the idea. These stools also make delightful small tables, or they can be stacked to hold magazines or remote control devices.

Pair of bamboo horseshoe arm chairs.

Unfortunately, the Chinese somehow neglected to associate high rank with high comfort and did not produce their own version of an overstuffed chair. Some Chinese chairs, though, are actually quite comfortable. Those with a horseshoe-shaped (a Western moniker) back coax the spine into a languid slouch that virtually defies any effort to work. When fashioned from bamboo, such chairs often provide a splat that comes right up and hugs the lower back. Similarly, yoke back chairs often have a curved vertical support that links nicely with the lumbar.

Otherwise, Chinese chairs have a decidedly Confucian posture. Confucius taught that there is only one proper course of action in a civilized society, and it involves strict moral parameters on relationships between father and son, husband and wife, subjects and rulers – in other words, the philosophical equivalent of sitting up straight.

Official's hat chairs – with a square back, horizontal top rail that extends beyond the back posts and squared horizontal arms that protrude over the front posts – don't offer much in the way of comfort, nor do their southern cousins, the southern official's hat chairs, whose notable difference is horizontal arms that do not extend over the front posts. By the way, the use of the term "official's hat chair" is apparently a modern Chinese one, probably taken from the fact that the backs of these chairs resemble the hats worn by government officials.

Craig Clunas, in *Chinese Furniture,* notes that they may have been called meditation chairs, but he also appropriately indicates that nomenclature doesn't really matter as much as design. He refers to "striking modernity in the simplicity and balance of their lines,"

which explains why these chairs are so popular in Western homes. They offer the quintessential example of the refinement that is Chinese furniture making. Their appearance almost suggests the Art Deco period, while at the same time calling up classical shapes – the wonderful juxtaposition of straight line and curve. We have seen chairs that clearly demonstrated a sense of whimsy, chairs that were rustic enough to display saw-tooth marks in unseen spots, and chairs with a highly polished, lacquered appearance and a wood grain that makes hard matter seem soft and warm – whatever the appearance, these chairs lend their room settings unquestionable elegance.

The chairs that Clunas writes about in his authoritative book date from the Ming and early Qing dynasties and might cost from $50,000 and up. A similar pair of chairs from the late Qing might cost $3,000 to $5,000. And to our taste, chairs from the late Qing are more interesting. With a clear finish, the elm has a richer, warmer grain, and in colors – black, black and red, red – they are wonderfully creative rather than auspiciously austere.

Other tables you might well find in this magnificent house – if your host decided to bring you past the reception hall and into the living quarters – would be work-related: a bright, red three or four drawer desk, for example, where correspondence might be undertaken and the family books balanced with an abacus stored in a nearby cabinet. Other work tables might include a painting table, some 34 inches tall, 20 inches deep, and 7 feet long. If your host were an educated man, he would surely indulge his creative urges by painting landscapes and village scenes on wide silk scrolls, rolled out flat on

Red lacquer 3 drawer desk with horse hoof legs.

the table while he stood above (unfortunately, only your host would have likely fanned such creative spark. Women, in this male-dominated society, did not paint, nor did they attend school.)

And if you had a Western decorator's eye, you might look at the painting table and realize that such a long, shallow table works well in the small dining room of a New York apartment, stored against one wall and brought out when the occasion warrants – your own version of the Eight Immortals table and a very Chinese approach to home furnishing. Because while the Chinese had specific uses intended for certain pieces of furniture, they had a penchant for practicality and were not at all shy about rearranging the rules on decorating.

Curiously, by Western standards, the room in this house with the greatest attention to interior design would be the gentleman's study. Most likely adjoining his bedroom, the study is the place where the master practices gentlemanly arts – reading, writing, painting, playing music, composing poetry, and studying antiques. (The Four Treasures of the study were a brush, ink, ink slab, and writing paper.) The central feature in your host's study would probably have been the day

bed, *ta*. Not really a bed so much as an elevated platform, the *ta* would have been about 6 feet long, 2 feet deep and 20 inches high with a cane top for comfortable sitting. A gentleman would sit on the day bed and engage in conversation, write poetry, or meditate on the nature of life. From it, he might look out on the adjoining garden with its delicate arrangements of rocks and trees, or he might gaze at a piece of sculpture displayed on a small bench. From the vantage point of an Internet-activated Western society, it seems wondrous to imagine a culture that placed its highest values on such pursuits.

And isn't that much of the appeal of these antiques? We live in a society that values speed and efficiency above almost all else. We seek instant gratification, computers that are seconds faster than their predecessors, and a virtual lifestyle that can be double-clicked into reality. Yet here was a society that cherished examining antiques, studying the crackled lacquer on an old cabinet, appreciating the delicate weave of a food basket. This was a society that focused much of its intellectual resources on the display of beautiful things. No wonder Westerners regarded China as a superior society.

Elmwood daybed.

ACCESSORIES

Accessories, perhaps more than anything else, tell the story of daily life in the Qing dynasty and the unique sense of form that makes Chinese antiques so compelling and delightful.

Baskets, jewelry boxes, food containers, lunch boxes, birdcages, calligraphy brushes, brush pots, rice baskets … there is a rich variety of these smaller items and they speak volumes.

Rice containers, for example, come in several sizes and shapes, often with painted exteriors. Red wedding baskets were taken to a bride on her wedding day and contained food or a small gift. Rice baskets with a thick weave transported grain from the market. And birdcages came in small, delicate sizes for grandfathers to take their pet birds out for a daily walk.

Document boxes designed to double as pillows tell us something of the dangers of travel in China.

These boxes let travelers sleep on their valuables. Clever jewelry boxes could open to reveal both a hidden mirror and hidden compartments to store valuables.

And leather boxes made to hold a lady's hair ornaments or accessories were often painted with scenes of children at play or groups of ladies at their leisure.

But more than utility, these accessories display wonderful shapes. The wedding baskets with hourglass handles. The rice measures shaped somewhat like a beehive. Necklace boxes in the form of a donut! Words fall short in these descriptions, so peruse through the photographs of some of our favorites. And imagine them on tabletops, on the floor in the corner of the living room, flanking a sideboard in the dining room, accenting a bookshelf almost anywhere.

CHAPTER 6

CABINETS

Detail of book cabinet.

Narrow, red lacquer book
cabinet with circle
hardware, elmwood, ca.
1820, 6' h. $3500-$5000.

Original hardware on book cabinet.

Black lacquer cabinet with gold paint design, scalloped hardware, elmwood, ca. 1850, 6' h. $5500-$7500.

Above: One of a pair of black lacquer cabinets with painted design, fancy hardware, and carved base, elmwood, ca. 1870, 6' h. $4500-$6500.

Right: Second of a pair of black lacquer cabinets with painted design, fancy hardware, and carved base, elmwood, ca. 1870, 6' h. $4500-$6500.

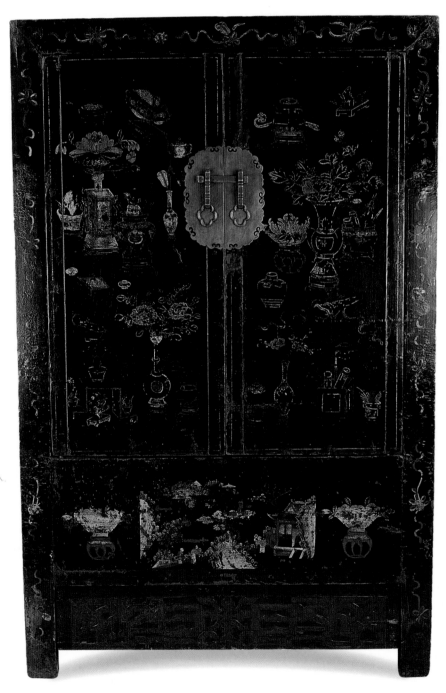

Left: Black lacquer cabinet with gold paint, 2 outside drawers, round hardware, elmwood, ca. 1870, 6' h. $5500-$7500.

Below: Detail of black lacquer cabinet.

Above: Red lacquer cabinet with gold paint design, curved bases and square hardware, elmwood, ca. 1850, 6' h. $5500-$7500.

Right: Detail of red lacquer cabinet.

Detail of red
lacquer cabinet.

Above: One of a pair of maroon lacquer cabinets with gold paint and carved base, bar-style hardware, elmwood, ca. 1860, 6' h. $5000-$7000.

Right: Detail of maroon lacquer cabinet.

Left: Matching pair to maroon lacquer cabinet.

Below left: Black lacquer cabinet with gold paint design and scalloped hardware, elmwood, ca. 1850, 6' h. $5500-$7500.

Below right: Detail of black lacquer cabinet.

Above: Black lacquer cabinet with gold paint design, 2 outside drawers and scalloped hardware, elmwood, ca. 1850, 6' h. $5500-$7500.

Right: Detail of black lacquer cabinet.

Left: Red lacquer A-line cabinet with humpback stretcher at base, 2 outside drawers and butterfly hardware, elmwood, ca. 1890, 5.5' h. $3000-$4000.

Below: Detail of butterfly hardware.

Above: Red lacquer wedding cabinet with large circle hardware and curved spandrels at the legs, elmwood, ca. 1890-1910, 5.5' h. $2500-$4500.

Above right: Detail of pulls on red wedding cabinet.

Lower right: Detail of etching on circle hardware on red wedding cabinet.

Above: Red lacquer wedding cabinet with small circle hardware and curved spandrels at the legs, elmwood, ca. 1890-1910, 5' h. $2500-$4000.

Right: Red lacquer wedding cabinet with fancy header, circle hardware, 2 outside drawers and carved detail at legs, elmwood, ca. 1890-1910, 5.5' h. $2500-$4000.

Below: Detail of header on red wedding cabinet.

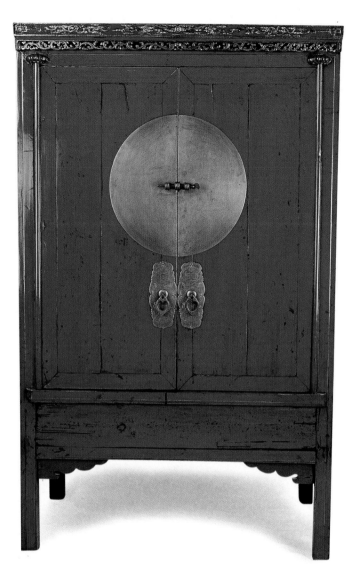

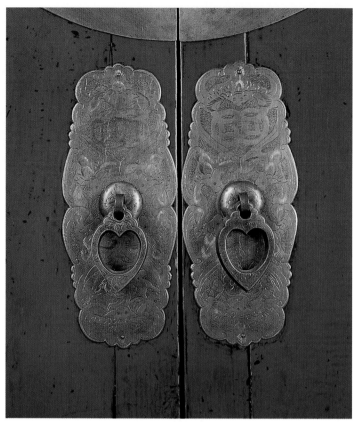

Left: Red lacquer wedding cabinet with fancy header and circle hardware, elmwood, ca. 1890-1910, 5.5' h. $2500-$4000.

Above: Detail of pulls on red wedding cabinet.

Below: Detail of header on red wedding cabinet.

Above right: Blackwood kitchen cabinet with carved upper doors, ca. 1880. 5.5' h. $3500-$5500.

Above left: Detail of carved doors on kitchen cabinet.

Right: Detail of inside upper door which has a closing panel to block sunlight when fruits and vegetables.

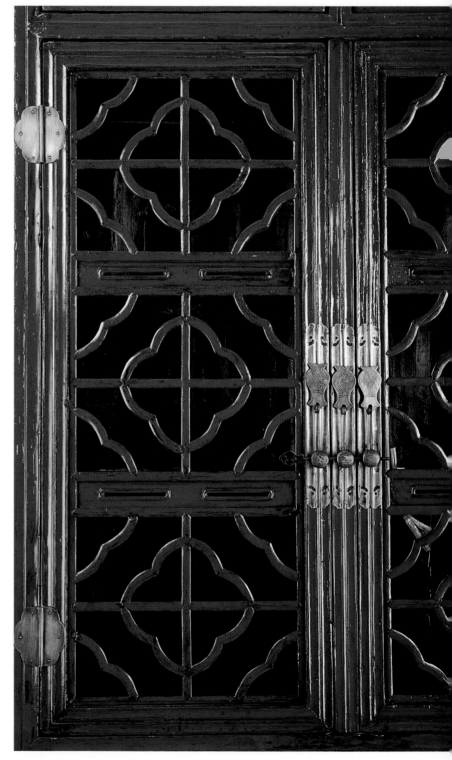

Above: Red lacquer kitchen cabinet with scalloped carving on upper doors and 4 outer drawers, elmwood, ca. 1880, 6' h. $3000-$5000.

Right: Detail of scalloped doors on kitchen cabinet.

Left: Brown lacquer kitchen cabinet with lattice doors, elmwood, ca. 1890, 6' h. $3500-$5500.

Above: Detail of carving on kitchen cabinet lattice doors.

Black lacquer kitchen cabinet with lattice doors, elmwood, ca. 1880, 6' h. $3000-$5000.

Red lacquer kitchen cabinet with glass upper doors and bone inlay, 2 outer drawers, elmwood, ca. 1920, 6' h. $2400-$3400.

Brown lacquer kitchen cabinet with spindle upper doors and 2 outer drawers, elmwood, ca. 1900, 5.5' h. $2000-$3000.

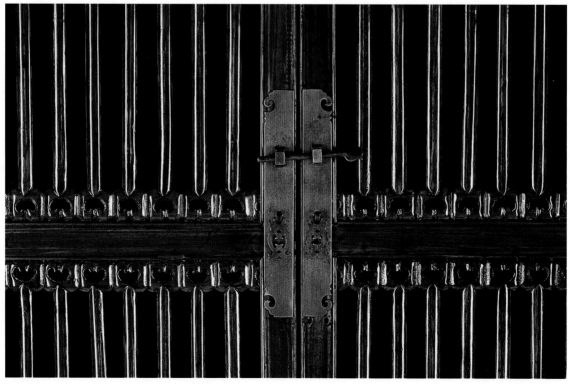

Detail of spindle doors on kitchen cabinet.

Detail of carved doors.

Elmwood cabinet with carved doors, 2 outer drawers,
humpback stretcher at base, ca. 1910. $3000-$5000.

Elmwood kitchen
cabinet with 8 doors
and 3 drawers, ca. 1880,
6' h. $2800-$4000.

Above: Elmwood kitchen cabinet with carved upper doors and 3 drawers, ca. 1880, 5.5' h. $2400-$4000.

Above right: Detail of carved doors on kitchen cabinet.

Right: Detail of lattice lower doors on kitchen cabinet.

Left: Black lacquer medicine/
herb cabinet with 42 divided
drawers, ca. 1860, 6' h.
$4000-$6500.

Below: Detail of front of herb
cabinet drawer with original
herb labels.

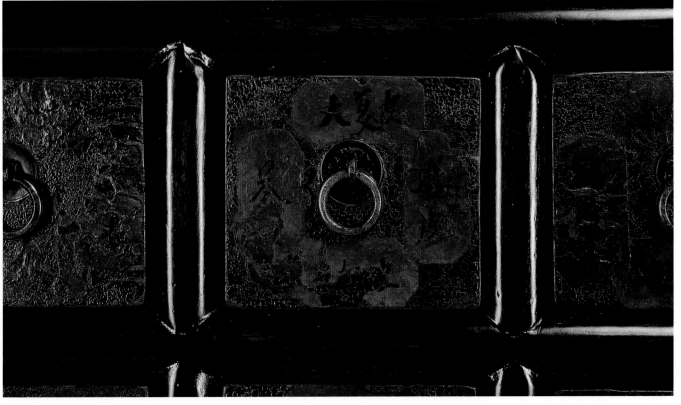

Above: Narrow Red Lacquer cabinet with 4 outer drawers and painting on the doors, ca. 1890, 5.5' h. $3500-$5500.

Right: Detail painting on door.

Above right: Red lacquer cabinet with elaborate carving and painting, 4 drawers, 4 doors, elmwood, ca. 1890, 6' h. ($3500-$5500).

Above left: Detail of painting on door.

Right: Detail of carving above door.

Red lacquer cabinet, 2 door with painting and hump-back stretcher at base, ca. 1890, 5.5' h. $2500-$4000.

Detail of painting on door.

Detail of painting and humpback stretcher.

Above: False 4 door red lacquer cabinet with carved detail at legs, elmwood, ca. 1890, 6' h. $3000-$5000.

Right: Half cabinet in red and black lacquer with gold painting, 2 drawers, 2 doors. Elmwood, ca. 1880, 3.5' h. $3800-$5800.

Below: Detail of painting on half cabinet.

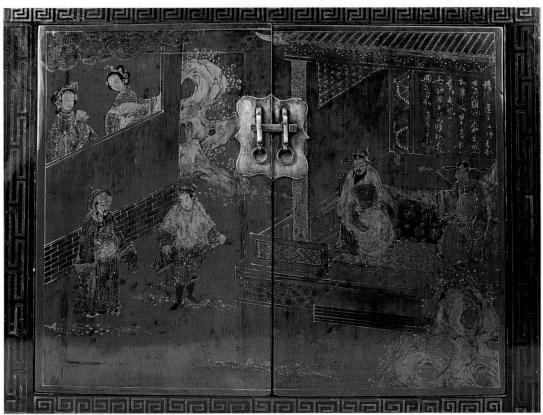

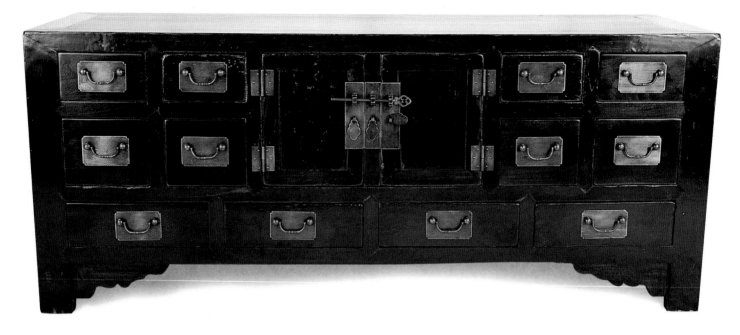

Kang cabinet in brown lacquer, 12 drawers, 2
doors, elmwood, ca. 1880, 2.5' h. $2500-$4000.

Kang cabinet in red lacquer 7 drawers, 4 doors,
elmwood, ca. 1880, 2.5' h. $2500-$4000.

Above: Double low cabinet in black lacquer with gold painting, 4 doors, elmwood, ca. 1880, 2.5' h. $2500-$3500.

Right: Detail of painting and hardware on double black cabinet.

Below: Detail of inside of double black cabinet.

Right: Small black lacquer cabinet with 2 red doors, elmwood, ca. 1870, 2.5' h. $2000-$4000.

Below: Detail of hardware and finish.

Above: Small red lacquer cabinet with gold painting and circle hardware, ca. 1880, 2.5' h. $1800-$3000.

Left: Detail of butterfly painting and hardware.

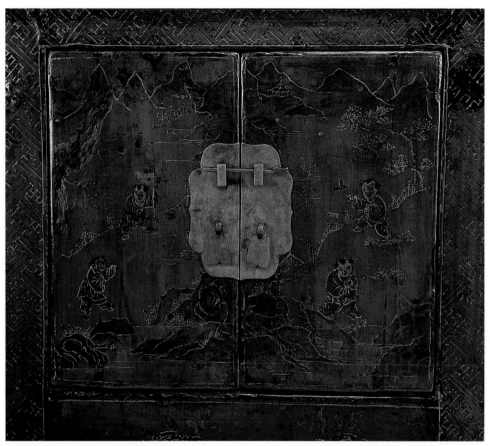

Detail of another small red lacquer cabinet
with different hardware and painting.

Detail of another small red lacquer
cabinet with different painting.

Detail of another small red lacquer cabinet
with different painting and hardware.

Above: Small black lacquer cabinet with gold painting, elmwood, ca. 1880, 2.5' h. $2500-$3500.

Left: Detail of gold painting and hardware.

Red lacquer half-cabinet with 2 drawers and 2
doors, elmwood, ca. 1890, 3' h. $2000-$3000.

Small A-line red lacquer cabinet with 2 drawers
and 2 doors, elmwood, ca. 1890, 3' h. $1600-$3000.

Above: Double black lacquer cabinet with gold painting with 4 drawers and 4 doors, elmwood, ca. 1880, 3.5' h. $4000-$5000.

Below: Detail of gold painting and hardware on double black cabinet.

Left: Small bamboo cabinet with 2 doors, ca. 1900, 4' h. $1200-$2000.

Above: Detail of bamboo doors.

Right: Small two-tone elmwood cabinet with 1 drawer and 2 doors, ca. 1910, 3' h. $1500-$2000.

Half cabinet in brown lacquer with 2 drawers, 2 doors and butterfly hardware, elmwood, ca. 1890, 3' h. $1500-$2300.

Left: Eight door cabinet with 4 drawers, Chinese characters and floral design, elmwood, ca. 1890, 6' h. $2400-$3600.

Below right: Eight door cabinet with 4 drawers, painting on each of the doors, elmwood, ca. 1880, 6' h. $3500-$5500.

Below left: Detail of painting on eight door cabinet.

Eight door cabinet
with 4 drawers,
painting on each of
the doors,
elmwood, ca. 1880,
6' h. $3500-$5500.

Above: Detail of drawer on eight door cabinet.

Left: Detail of painting on eight door cabinet.

Above: False 4 door cabinet with gold painting, humpback stretcher at base, elmwood, ca. 1880, 6' h. $3000-$5000.

Right: Ningbo cabinet, rosewood, cypress and elmwood, with bone inlay, 3 drawers, ca. 1890, 5.5' h. $3500-$4500.

Below: Detail of drawer of Ningbo cabinet.

Two-piece Ningbo cabinet with 2 drawers, 4 doors, elmwood, rosewood, blackwood, ca. 1900. $3.500-$5500.

Detail of drawer hardware on Ningbo cabinet.

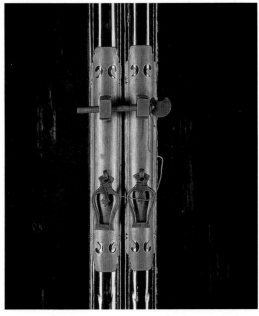

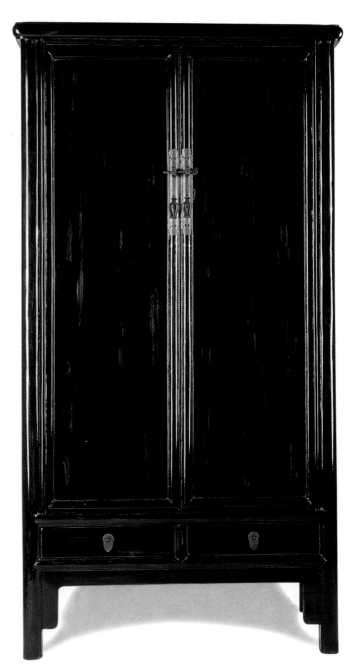

Above left: Square corner, 2 door elmwood cabinet, ca. 1880, 6' h. $3000-$5000.

Above right: Square corner, black lacquer cabinet with 2 outer drawers, ca. 1880, 6' h. $3000-$5000.

Left: Detail of hardware on black lacquer cabinet.

Above: Maroon lacquer cabinet with carved base, double pin, elmwood, ca. 1850, 6' h. $3500-$6000.

Right: Tapered elmwood cabinet with 2 doors, ca. 1880, 6' h. $3000-$4500.

CHAPTER 7

CHAIRS AND STOOLS

Pair of bamboo horseshoe arm chairs with
elm wood seats, ca. 1840. $2000-$4000.

Right: Pair of bamboo horseshoe back arm chairs with cane seats, ca. 1820. $2000-$4000.

Below: Pair of elmwood horseshoe arm chairs, ca. 1880. $2000-$4000.

Left: Blackwood horseshoe armchair with carved back splat, carved skirt and curved side supports, ca. 1880. $2000-$4000.

Below left: Detail of carved back splat on blackwood armchair.

below right: Detail of arm on blackwood armchair.

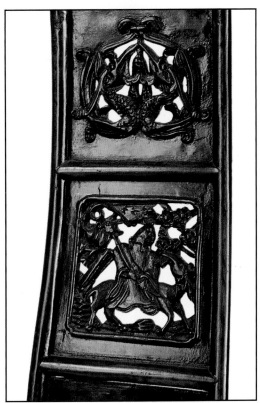

Pair of red lacquer official's hat chairs with cane seats, straight headrests and curved side supports, elmwood, ca. 1880. $2000-$4000.

Pair of black lacquer official's hat chairs with yoke back headrests, curved side supports and cane seats, elmwood, ca. 1860. $2000-$4000

Pair of brown lacquer official's hat chairs with curved side supports and cane seats, elmwood, ca. 1880. $2000-$4000.

Pair of square back bamboo armchairs with elmwood seats, ca. 1880. $2000-$4000.

Blackwood armchair with carving on back splat and curved side supports, cane seat, ca. 1900. $1000-$2000.

Pair of square back bamboo
armchairs with elmwood seats,
ca. 1880. $2000-$4000.

Pair of maroon lacquer, spindle
back armchairs with cane seats,
ca. 1880. $2000-$4000.

Small bamboo armchair
with spindle back and
arms and round elmwood
seat, ca. 1900. $900-$1800.

Left: Pair of black lacquer six corner chairs with curved side supports and carved back splats, elmwood, ca. 1880. $2000-$4000.

Below: Detail of carved back splat on six corner chairs.

Red lacquer
wedding chair
with carved,
curved back splat,
carving between
and down front
legs, one drawer,
elmwood, ca.
1870. $900-$1800.

Side shot of wedding
chair showing drawer
and curved back splat.

Detail of carving in back
splat of wedding chair.

Above: Reddish-brown lacquer wedding chair with carved detail between front legs and carving on back splat, elmwood, ca. 1880. $900-$1800.

Right: Detail of carving on back splat of wedding chair.

Above: Red lacquer wedding chair with carved and cut out back splat and one drawer, elmwood, ca. 1880. $900-$1800.

Right: Detail of carved and cut out back splat of wedding chair.

Elmwood and cane resting chair with built-in pillow and retractable footrest, ca. 1890. $1000-$2000.

Blackwood resting chair with cutout back and curved arms, ca. 1910. $1000-$2000.

Bamboo resting chair with adjustable back and built in pillow, ca. 1900. $1000-$2000.

Child's high chair with movable tray and removable cane seat, elmwood and cane, ca. 1920. $1000-$2000.

Child's high chair with spindle back and arms, elmwood, ca. 1920. $900-$1800.

Child's walker on wheels with tray and lattice design, elmwood, ca. 1920. $1000-$2000.

Pair of round top stools,
elmwood, ca. 1880.
$700-$1400.

Brown lacquer
elmwood bench with
solid top, ca. 1880.
$900-$1800.

Rectangular stool with
humpback stretcher and
horsehoof legs, blackwood,
ca. 1870. $700-$1500

Small square stool with
one drawer and
horsehoof legs,
elmwood, ca. 1880.
$500-$1200

Above: Pair of rectangular stools
with decorative brace and horsehoof
legs, ca. 1880. $900-$1200

Right: Detail of decorative brace.

Pair of red lacquer, square stools with straight supports, reeded molding, and hump-back stretcher, cane top, ca. 1890. $1500-$2500.

Pair of red lacquer square stools with double circle supports and humpback stretchers, cane top, ca. 1890. $1500-$2500.

Pair of square-top stools with decorative brace, humpback stretchers and cane top, ca. 1890. $1500-$2500.

Pair of square-top elmwood stools with cane top and hump-back stretchers, stripped of their original color, ca. 1900. $1000-$2000.

Set of 4 rectangular stools, with humpback stretchers and reeded molding, ca. 1890. $2400-$3400

Elmwood footrest with lattice top, ca. 1870. $500-$1000.

Detail of top of footrest

Elmwood footrest with horsehoof legs, ca. 1880. $500-$1000.

Workman's stool with two drawers,
elmwood, ca. 1870. $800-$1600.

Cobbler's bench with one drawer,
elmwood, ca. 1870. $500-$1000.

Small, square red lacquer stool with one drawer
and horsehoof legs, ca. 1880. $500-$1000.

Peachwood bench with cane top, horsehoof legs, and "5 precious pearls" design on recessed waist with carved spandrels, ca. 1860. $800-$2000.

Detail of carved spandrel.

Detail of "5 precious pearls" design on recessed waist.

Above: Elmwood bench with everted ends, carved spandrels merging into a carved waist, and carving on panel between side legs, ca. 1870. $1500-$3000.

Left: Detail of carved spandrel and waist.

Below: Detail of carving between side legs.

CHAPTER 8

TABLES

Elmwood altar table with everted ends and
carved spandrels, ca. 1860. $2500-$5000.

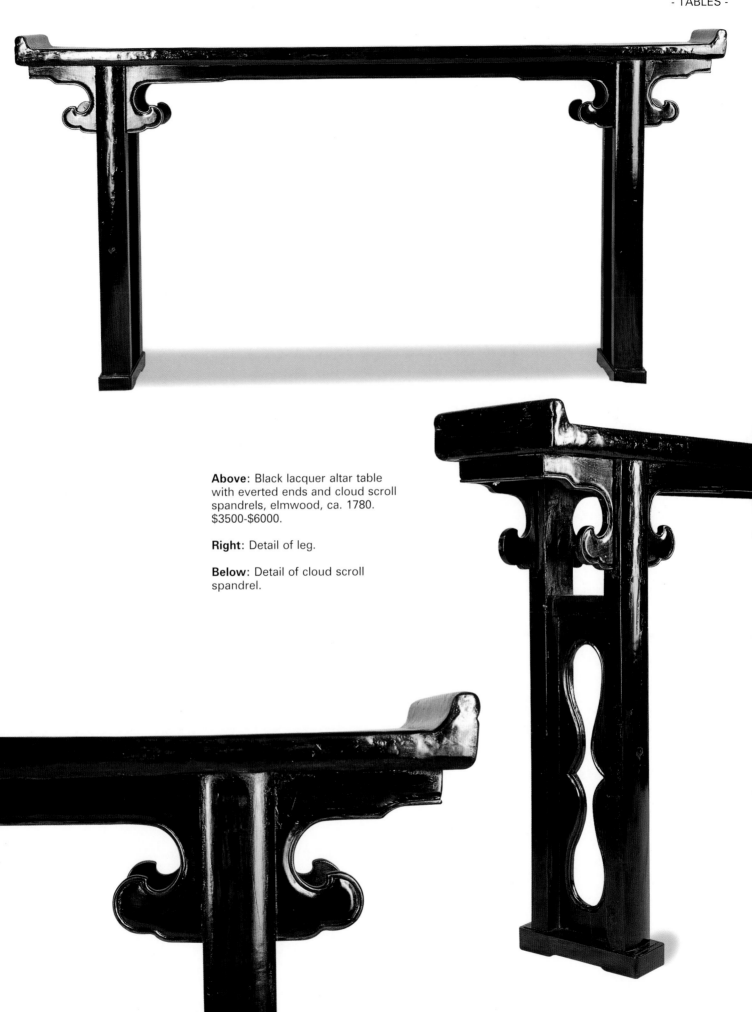

Above: Black lacquer altar table with everted ends and cloud scroll spandrels, elmwood, ca. 1780. $3500-$6000.

Right: Detail of leg.

Below: Detail of cloud scroll spandrel.

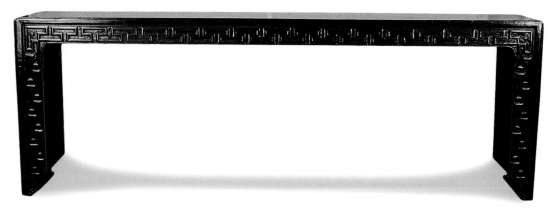

Blackwood altar
table, ca. 1860.
$5000-$7000.

Bamboo and elmwood
altar table in red lacquer
with 2 drawers, ca. 1880.
$2000-$4000.

Detail of bamboo detail on red lacquer table.

Above: Small red lacquer altar table with everted ends and cloud scroll spandrels, elmwood, ca. 1880. $1600-$3200.

Right: Small altar table with everted ends, 2 drawers and lower shelf, with carved waist and spandrels, elmwood, ca. 1870. $1600-$3200.

Below: Red lacquer altar coffer table with 3 drawers and carved spandrels, elmwood, ca. 1890. $2000-$4000.

Top: Small blackwood altar table with humpback stretcher, ca. 1860. $1800-$3600.

Center: Elmwood wine table with reeded molding and vertical supports, ca. 1860. $1800-$3600.

Bottom: Elmwood wine table with "S" curve braces and horse hoof legs, ca. 1860. $1800-$3600.

Above: Elmwood side table with carved drop waist,
hidden drawer, and horsehoof legs, ca. 1850. $2000-$3500.

Below: Detail of carved waist.

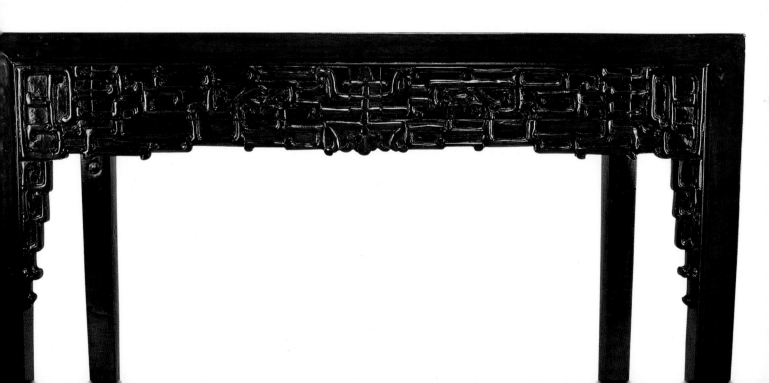

Above: Elmwood side table with decorative spandrels and horizontal front and back supports, ca. 1870. $1800-$3600.

Right: Red lacquer coffer table with carved and gilded drawers, elmwood, ca. 1880. $2000-$3000.

Red lacquer gate leg table with one drawer, elmwood, ca. 1920. $1000-$2000.

Elmwood demi-lune table in black and brown lacquer with semicircular base stretcher, drop waist with carving and cloud scrolls, chi dragon design on feet, ca. 1870. $2000-$4000.

Above: Round table which comes apart as 2 demilune tables, black and brown lacquer, elmwood, scalloped waist, scallop detail on legs, triangular base stretcher and horsehoof legs, ca. 1870. $3500-$5000.

Right: Six-corner bamboo table with vertical supports and hexagonal base stretcher, ca. 1860. $2000-$3000.

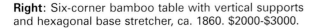

Above: Blackwood gate leg game table with removable top and 4 drawers, ca. 1870. $2500-$3500.

Left: Eight Immortals table with carved spandrels, elmwood, ca. 1850. $2000-$4000.

Below: Detail of carved spandrel.

Above: Red lacquer kang table with 3 drawers, "5 precious pearls" design on waist , horsehoof legs, elmwood, ca. 1880. $2200-$3500.

Below: Elmwood daybed with vertical supports and cane top, ca. 1820. $3000-$5000.

Above: Red lacquer kang table with brown top, horsehoof legs, 2 drawers, elmwood, ca. 1890. $2200-$3500.

Right: Detail of hardware on kang table.

Above: Red lacquer kang table with 3 drawers, butterfly hardware on one drawer, horsehoof legs, elmwood, ca. 1890. $2200-$3500.

Right: Detail of butterfly hardware.

Top: Brown lacquer kang table with 4 drawers, horsehoof legs, elmwood, ca. 1890. $2200-$3500.

Center: Brown lacquer painting table cut down to kang table size, recessed legs, elmwood, ca. 1860. $2500-$3500.

Bottom: Black lacquer, 3 drawer kang table with recessed waist and horsehoof legs, elmwood, ca. 1870. $2200-$3500.

Top: Square, brown lacquer kang table, 4 drawers, reeded molding, elmwood, ca. 1890. $2200-$3000.

Bottom: Detail of grain pattern in top of square kang table.

Square red and brown lacquer kang table with 2 drawers and horsehoof legs, elmwood, ca. 1890. $2200-$3500.

Rectangular red and brown lacquer kang table with large horse hoof legs, recessed waist, elmwood, ca. 1850. $2200-$3200.

Square, brown lacquer kang table with recessed waist, humpback stretcher, horsehoof legs, elmwood with burlwood center, ca. 1870. $2800-$3600.

Rectangular bamboo kang table with black elmwood top, ca. 1860. $2200-$3500.

Brown lacquer kang table with recessed waist, 2 drawers, horsehoof legs, ca. 1880. $2200-$3500.

Elmwood kang table with recessed waist, black lacquer legs and brown lacquer top, horsehoof legs, ca. 1870. $900-$2200.

Top: Bamboo and
elmwood kang table
with fret work,
ca. 1850. $1500-$2500.

Center: Elmwood lap
table with carved waist
and spandrels and
hidden drawer,
ca. 1850. $800-$2000.

Bottom: Elmwood
kang table with reeded
molding, two drawers
ca. 1870. $700-$1400.

Bamboo kang table with
one drawer, ca. 1860.
$700-$1400.

Above: Elmwood 5-part
scholar's desk with 10 drawers,
ca. 1880. $3500-$6000.

Right: Detail of hardware and
connection of center piece to
side piece.

Above: Brown lacquer desk with recessed waist, 3 drawers, butterfly hardware on center drawer, horsehoof legs, ca. 1870. $2000-$3500.

Left: Detail of butterfly hardware.

Below: Bamboo desk with lattice footrest, 2 drawers, black lacquer elmwood top, ca. 1850. $2000-$4000.

Above: Red lacquer 3 drawer desk with horse hoof legs, elmwood, ca. 1870. $2400-$4000.

Right: Detail of drawer on red lacquer desk.

Below: Brown lacquer desk with 5 drawers. Elmwood, horsehoof legs, ca. 1880. $3200-$6000.

Brown lacquer coffer desk (hidden compartment beneath drawers) with 3 drawers, horsehoof legs, elmwood, ca. 1870. $2400-$4000.

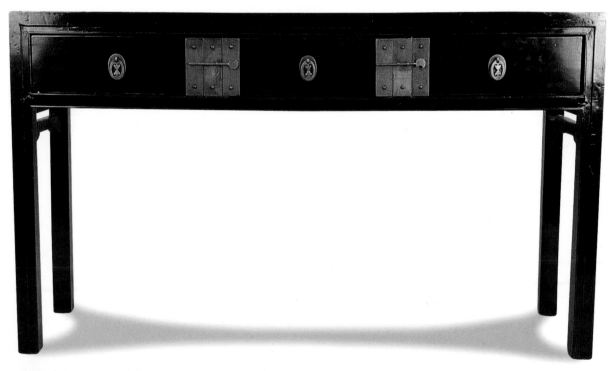

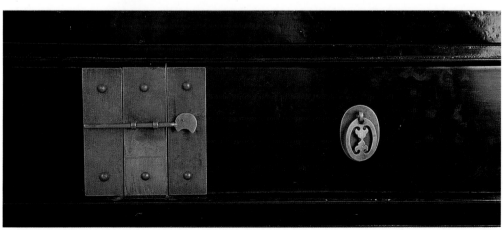

Above: Black lacquer desk with 3 drawers and 2 locks, horsehoof legs, ca. 1860. $3200-$6000.

Left: Detail of lock on black lacquer desk.

Above: Red lacquer desk with 5 drawers and butterfly hardware, horsehoof legs, elmwood, ca. 1890. $1800-$3600.

Below: Detail of butterfly hardware on red lacquer desk.

Right: Bamboo tea table with lower shelf, elmwood top, flared legs, ca. 1870. $1200-$2400.

Below: Brown lacquer occasional table with circle cutout and 4 bats design, reeded molding, elmwood, ca. 1880. $1200-$2400.

Below right: Detail of bat.

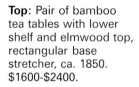

Top: Pair of bamboo tea tables with lower shelf and elmwood top, rectangular base stretcher, ca. 1850. $1600-$2400.

Bottom: Pair of elmwood tea tables with brown lacquer legs and black lacquer top, recessed waist, lower shelf, humpback stretcher at base, ca. 1860. $1800-$3000.

Left: Small chest of 13 drawers, elmwood, ca. 1870. $600-$1500.

Below: Small storage chest with 2 doors, 3 drawers and one hidden drawer, elmwood, ca. 1880. $400-$1000.

Mini-cabinet (14" high) with block feet and lotus detail on door hinge, elmwood, one drawer inside, ca. 1890. $350-$700.

Detail of interior of mini-cabinet.

Mini black lacquer altar coffer table (8" high) with everted ends, 2 doors and 2 drawers. Elmwood, ca. 1880. $700-$1000.

Small stand (4" high) with 4 drawers and carved
spandrels, elmwood, ca. 1870. $400-$1000.

Above: Black lacquer
food box with square
handle and chi
dragon design at
base of handle,
elmwood, ca. 1870.
$400-$700.

Left: Detail of chi
dragon design.

Red Lacquer food container with lid, elmwood, ca. 1880. $400-$600.

Red lacquer candy box with carving, elmwood, ca. 1870. $300-$500

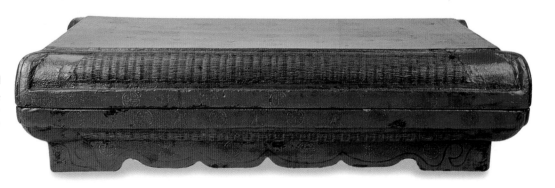

Red lacquer wood and cane storage box, elmwood, ca. 1870. $400-$800.

Brown lacquer wood and cane storage box with painted lid, ca. 1880. $400-$800.

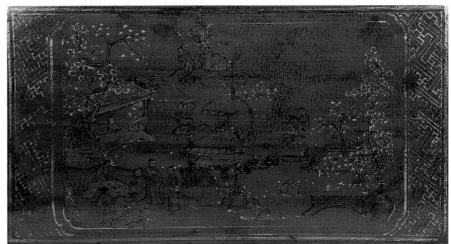

Detail of painted lid.

Above: Round wooden storage box with base, floral painted design, elmwood, ca. 1900. $400-$800.

Right: Detail of lid.

Right: Round woven storage basket with painted wooden frame, ca. 1870. $300-$700.

Below: Detail of painted wooden frame.

Above: Bamboo and cane oval storage basket with lid, square handle and decorative hardware, ca. 1870. $400-$900.

Right: Bamboo and cane storage basket with lid and rounded handle, ca. 1880. $300-$600.

Bamboo and cane round basket with base and hinged lid, ca. 1880. $350-$550.

Rectangular storage basket with hinged lid and square handle, ca. 1880. $400-$800.

Side view of rectangular basket.

Detail of weave on rectangular basket.

Top left: Three-layer wooden food basket with painted design, bamboo handle and decorative hardware (22" high), elmwood, ca. 1870. $575-$1000.

Above: Detail of painted design on side of food basket.

Left: Detail of painted design on lid of food basket.

Top: Pillow-shaped storage basket of cane and bamboo with hinged lid, ca. 1870. $350-$600.

Center: Detail of pattern on lid of "pillow" basket.

Right: Three-layer black and red lacquer food box with square handle and decorative hardware, ca. 1870. $400-$800.

Three-layer bamboo food box with yoke-shaped handle, ca. 1870. $350-$600.

Round wooden food box with lid, rounded handle, decorative hardware, painted design, elmwood, ca. $300-$600.

Small red lacquer food box with painted design (8" high), decorative hardware, ca. 1880. $200-$400.

Small red lacquer food box with painted design "8" high), ca. 1800. $200-$400.

Above: Round food box with painted lid, rounded handle and decorative hardware, elmwood, (12" high) ca. 1900. $300-$600.

Right: Two-layer hexagonal wooden food box with painted design, yoke-shaped handle and decorative hardware, elmwood, (14" high) ca. 1880. $300-$600.

Detail of painted lid of hexagonal box.

Maroon lacquer and gilt round food basket with rounded lid and tall rounded handles, elmwood, ca. 1870. $300-$500.

Maroon lacquer and gilt round food basket with rounded lid and tall rounded handles, elmwood, ca. 1870. $300-$500.

Red lacquer food bucket with lid and decorative handle, elmwood, ca. 1890. $260-$500.

Maroon lacquer and gilt round food basket with rounded lid and tall rounded handles, elmwood, ca. 1870. $300-$500.

Maroon lacquer round food basket with rounded lid and tall rounded handles, elmwood, ca. 1870. $300-$500.

Maroon lacquer and gilt round food basket with rounded lid and tall rounded handles, elmwood, ca. 1870. $300-$500.

Red lacquer food box with locking top, elmwood (16" high), ca. 1880. $300-$400.

Above: Pair of three-layer cane and bamboo food baskets with carrying baskets and pole, (36" high) ca. 1870. $1000-$3000.

Right: Red lacquer food box with carving and gold paint, locking handle, elmwood, ca. 1900. $300-$400.

Red lacquer wedding food box, 4 layers, carving and gold paint,
carrying pole, elmwood, (36" high), ca. 1910. $1500-$3000.

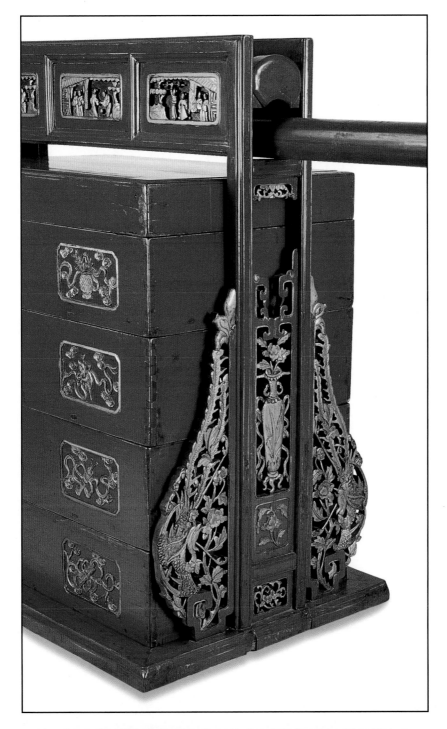

Above: Detail of side of wedding food box.

Left: Detail of carved handle on wedding food box.

Brown lacquer bamboo and
cane two-layer food basket
with square, locking handle,
ca. 1880. $300-$600.

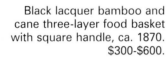

Black lacquer bamboo and
cane three-layer food basket
with square handle, ca. 1870.
$300-$600.

Cylindrical food basket
with lid and yoke-shaped
handle, cane and bamboo,
ca. 1890. $300-$600.

Above left: Two-layer bamboo and cane food basket with square handle and decorative hardware (24" high), ca. 1880. $350-$700.

Above right: Detail of weave on food basket.

Round red lacquer water bucket with narrow handle (16" high), elmwood, ca. 1890. $200-$400.

Round red lacquer water bucket with wide handle (16" high), elmwood, ca. 1890. $200-$400.

Above left: Oval red lacquer water bucket with carved handle (12" high), elmwood, ca. 1890. $300-$600.

Above right: Red lacquer wedding basket with curved handle, elmwood (14" high), ca. 1880. $200-$450.

Below left: Red lacquer wedding basket with hour glass handle, elmwood (12" high), ca. 1880. $200-$450.

Below right: Red lacquer wedding basket with black and gold carved handle, elmwood (12" high), ca. 1880. $250-$500.

Red lacquer wedding basket with carving and gold paint on handle, elmwood (14" high), ca. 1900. $250-$500.

Above: Round brown lacquer food box with gold dragons on handle, elmwood (10" high), ca. 1880. $250-$500.

Right: Detail of gold dragon.

Oval red lacquer wedding basket with carved, gilt handle, elmwood (12" high), ca. 1880. $250-$500.

Round red lacquer wedding basket with carved, gilt handle, carved lid, elmwood, (12" high), ca. 1880. $250-$500.

Round red lacquer wedding basket with dragons on handle and carved lid, elmwood (10" high), ca. 1880. $250-$500.

Bright red lacquer wedding basket with curved handle, elmwood, (10" high), ca. 1890. $200-$400.

Left: Red lacquer rice container with gold foo dog on lid, elmwood (9" high), ca. 1900. $200-$300.

Below: Black lacquer rice container with gold design and gold foo dog on lid, elmwood, ca. 1900. $200-$300.

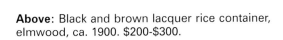

Above: Black and brown lacquer rice container, elmwood, ca. 1900. $200-$300.

Right: Brown lacquer rice container with circle hardware, elmwood, ca. 1900. $200-$300.

Above: Red lacquer elmwood bowl with brass bands (12" w), ca. 1880. $300-$600.

Right: Red lacquer elmwood bowl with brass bands and wide lip (18" w), ca. 1880. $300-$600.

Below: Brown lacquer elmwood basin with brass bands (20" w), ca. 1880. $300-$600.

Red and brown lacquer bowl, elmwood (12″ w), ca. 1880. $300-$600.

Above: Red lacquer elmwood basin with lid, (18″ w), ca. 1880. $300-$500.

Right: Rectangular cane and bamboo basket with red base, (12″ w), ca. 1880. $250-$400.

Right: Large oval cane and bamboo basket with fret work, (26" w), ca. 1880. $300-$500.

Below: Bottom view of oval basket.

Above: Bamboo and cane grain measure (24" high), ca. 1890. $300-$500.

Right: Detail of grain measure handle.

Below: Detail of weave on grain measure.

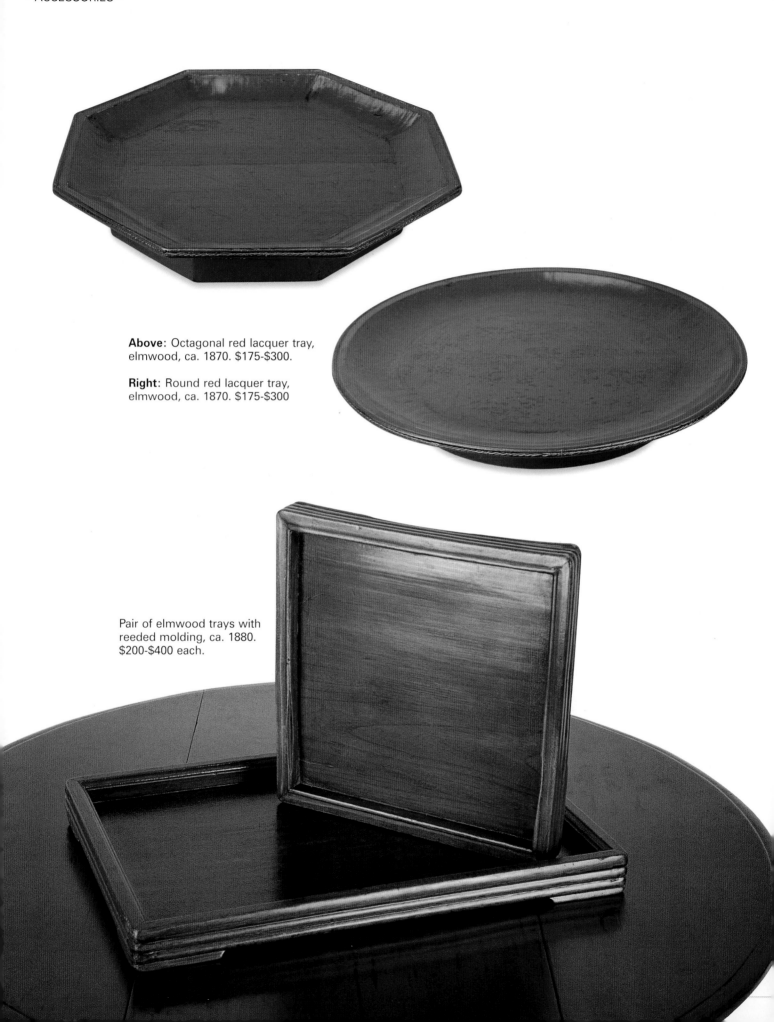

Above: Octagonal red lacquer tray, elmwood, ca. 1870. $175-$300.

Right: Round red lacquer tray, elmwood, ca. 1870. $175-$300

Pair of elmwood trays with reeded molding, ca. 1880. $200-$400 each.

Above: Rectangular red lacquer tray, elmwood, ca. 1870. $175-$300.

Right: Round tray with painting, elmwood, ca. 1870. $200-$300

Above: Rosewood and bone tray, ca. 1890. $200-$400

Right: Blackwood and bone tray, ca. 1890. $200-$400

Above: Rosewood jewelry box with mirrored and carved sides, stand-up mirror and 2 drawers (6' h), ca. 1900. $400-$800.

Right: Jewelry box with mirror standing.

Above: Blackwood jewelry box with stand-up mirror and 2 drawers, ca. 1900. $400-$800.

Left: Blackwood jewelry box with mirror standing.

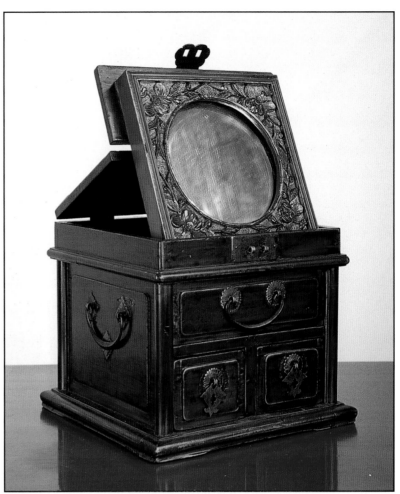

Above: Elmwood jewelry box with stand-up mirror and 3 drawers, ca. 1900. $400-$800

Right: Elmwood jewelry box with mirror standing.

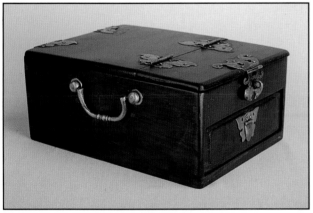

Above: Blackwood jewelry box with stand-up mirror and one drawer, ca. 1900. $400-$600.

Right: Blackwood jewelry box with mirror standing.

Above: Large black lacquer and gilt jewelry box with 2 doors and 5 drawers, elmwood, ca. 1880. $700-$900.

Left: Inside of large jewelry box.

Elmwood with bone inlay jewelry box with doweled lid and one drawer, ca. 1870. $300-$600.

Top: Red leather scholar's box with embossed and gilt design (12" x 3"), ca. 1870. $350-$500.

Center: Brown leather scholar's box, ca. 1880. $300-$400.

Bottom: Brown leather scholar's box with embossed and painted design (14" x 9"), ca. 1880. $300-$600.

Above: Black leather scholar's box with gilt painting (12" x 8") ca. 1880. $300-$600.

Below: Gilt painting on lid of black leather scholar's box.

Brown leather scholar's box
with painted design (12" x
8"), ca. 1880. $300-$600.

Gilt painting on lid
of brown leather
scholar's box.

Brown leather scholar's box
with faded design (14" x
11"), ca. 1880. $400-$600.

Faded design on
inside lid of brown
leather´scholar's box.

Brown leather scholar's box with two gold dragons ((14" x 11"), ca. 1890. $400-$800.

Brown leather suitcase (24" x 6"), ca. 1890. $400-$800.

Red wooden trunk with gilt design and butterfly hardware on stand, elmwood (36" x 18"), ca. 1890. $1000-$1800.

Black wooden trunk with gilt design on stand,
elmwood, (36" x 18"), ca. 1870. $800-$2000.

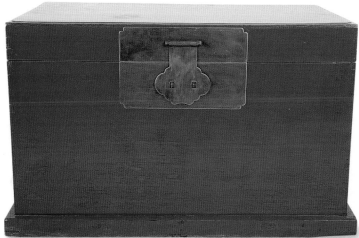

Red wooden trunk with base,
elmwood, (36" x 25"), ca. 1880.
$1200-$2000.

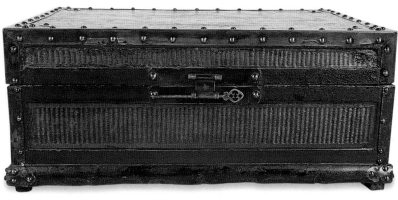

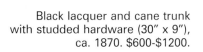

Black lacquer and cane trunk
with studded hardware (30" x 9"),
ca. 1870. $600-$1200.

Above: Red leather trunk with gilt design (36" x 14"), ca. 1870. $800-$2000.

Right: Detail of gilt design on red trunk.

Red leather trunk with rounded lid, embossed and gilt design, (36" x 14"), ca. 1870. $800-$2000.

Left: Detail of bat design on lid of red leather trunk.

Below: Detail of auspicious symbols embossed on red leather trunk.

Brown leather trunk with artist's chop (signature in the form of a seal) on front, (30" x 16"), ca. 1870. $400-$900.

Detail of artist's chop.

Pair of black lacquer elmwood storage boxes, (22" x 22"), ca. 1890. $800-$1000 each.

Summer mandarin's hat with
faded red tassels and brass finial
(8" high), ca. 1870. $700-$1000.

Summer mandarin's hat with red tassels
and crystal finial, ca. 1870. $700-$1000.

Summer mandarin's hat with red tassels
and bone finial, ca. 1870. $700-$1000.

Top: Winter mandarin's hat with red tassels and brass finial (6" high), ca. 1870. $450-$900.

Above: Child's mandarin hat with red beaded finial (4" high), 1870. $400-$800.

Right: Brown leather cylindrical hat box (15" high), ca. 1870. $400-$800.

Above: Double black leather hat box, ca. 1870. $450-$900.

Left: Double red leather hat box to hold summer and winter hats (16" high), ca. 1870. $450-$900.

Above: Cylindrical wooden hat box with painted and gilt design. (15" high), ca. 1880. $400-$800.

Left: Detail of gilt design on lid of wooden hat box.

Huanghuali brush pot and burlwood and
horsehair calligraphy brush, ca. 1870.
$500-$1000 brush pot; $400-$800 brush.

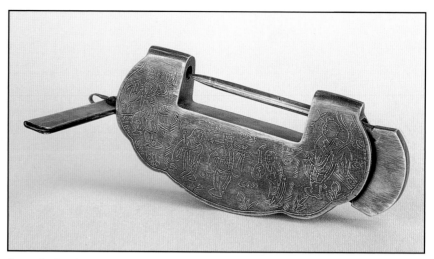

Brass lock with engraving (5" long),
ca. 1890. $150-$200.

Pair of red drums, (12" high),
ca. 1920. $200-$400 pair

Carved bamboo
brush pot, ca. 1890.
$300-$600.

Above: Red lacquer robe stand,
elmwood (48" high), ca. 1880.
$700-$1000.

Left: Pendulum clock with
worked brass work in dragon
motif around glass, (14" high),
ca. 1920. $500-$800.

Left: Bamboo chicken basket, (14" high), ca. 1910. $300-$500.

Below: Baby's toilet, removable half lid, elmwood, ca. 1910. $300-$600.

Bottom: Locking money box, elmwood, (12" high), ca. 1920. $300-$600.

Clockwise from top left:
Bamboo pillow, ca. 1920. $200-$300.

Maroon and red lacquer leather pillow,
(9" long), ca. 1880. $300-$600.

Two-part red lacquer baby bath,
elmwood (16" high), ca. 1880. $400-$800.

Elmwood juice presser, (18" high),
ca. 1890. $300-$600.

Above right: Locking money box, elmwood, (13" high), ca. 1890. $400-$800.

Above: Elmwood cooking table, (20" high) , ca. 1900. $400-$800.

Right: Bamboo bird cage, (18" high), ca. 1880. $400-$800.

Detail of handle on bird cage.

Above left: Bamboo birdcage, (18" high), ca. 1880. $600-$1000.

Above right: Detail of handle on birdcage.

Left: Round blackwood birdcage with porcelain dishes, bone perch, (10" high), ca. 1910. $800-$1200.

Round bamboo birdcage, ca. 1910. $300-$400.

Detail of birdcage door.

Bamboo bed with built-in pillow
(50" long), ca. 1910. $600-$1200.

DECORATING WITH CHINESE ANTIQUES

A beautiful maroon lacquer cabinet, with a silk tassel hanging from the pin, is used for clothes storage. Also, two small elmwood cabinets with removable doors, which reveal an interior shelf and drawers, serve well as night stands or bedside tables (only one showing on left side of bed)

Left: A one-of-a-kind, false four door elmwood cabinet with inlaid mother-of-pearl and gold painted design of birds, flowers and Chinese characters, is used for clothing storage. The pillow basket on top is for decoration only.

Below: This elmwood side table, with two drawers and carved spandrels, is used as a TV stand. A Chinese birdcage is to the right of the TV and two food baskets of different shapes and sizes are on the floor to the left.

Above: A stunning 18th century altar table sits astride a 20th century carved Chinese trunk made for export. A 2000-year-old terra cotta head of a Han dynasty warrior graces the top of the altar table.

OPPOSITE PAGE:

Top: A 19th century gold painted black lacquer trunk gets a new stand and is used as an end table between two couches. On top is a red lacquer wedding basket.

Bottom: A small 19th century kang table with reeded molding is used as a display table at the end of a couch.

A beautiful 19th century red lacquer bowl
graces a modern dining table and chairs.

An elmwood and cane rice container, a leather
scholar's box, and a red lacquer food basket
are ornaments on a modern glass coffee table.

Opposite page: A fancy wedding chair, tea table, and two food baskets go nicely with this American painting and drop leaf table.

Left: A tea table and a painted food basket fill this space below a hallway mirror.

Below: A square coffee table serves both couches in this family room.

Above: A red lacquer stool is the perfect accent table between two white chairs.

Left: Two red leather pillows add interest to this vase of hydrangeas on a round foyer table.

Opposite page: A stack of elmwood plates is the perfect addition to this collection of international antiques.

On Page 174: A gorgeous early 19th century cabinet with crackled red lacquer finish is the focal point at the base of the stairway in a lovely foyer.

The type and quality of woods plays as important a role in antique Chinese furniture as it does in Western pieces, sometimes more so. Identical tables, for example, from the same region and the same period but made from different types of woods can have different prices – differences that could put two extra zeros in front of the decimal point.

We found a coffee table in a friend's home that was made from *zitan*, not the traditional southern elm of the late Qing dynasty. She had bought it at a garage sale for $30. Its value could well be $10,000, because not only is *zitan* a hardwood that somehow feels buttery soft, it is extinct.

But all the woods used in Chinese furniture are beautiful to look at and touch. The Chinese usually selected woods with vivid grains and warm hues. This is an important feature even in furniture that has been colored. One of the attractions of these antiques is pieces with worn down finishes that reveal the bare wood beneath. The juxtaposition of wood and color creates a warm textured finish that is highly desirable.

What follows is a list of the woods you might expect, or hope, to find in late Qing pieces, plus a couple of extras, notably *zitan*, which had apparently vanished from the planet by the time the late Qing furniture makers picked up their planes.

Zitan (Zee-tahn): The most sought after wood of the Chinese court, it was imported from southeast Asia and cut to extinction. It is a very hard wood and thought to be a yellow flower pear wood. It has a rich, deep purple/black color. Once you've laid a hand to *zitan*, you'll always be able to identify it by touch.

Huanghuali (Wong-wah-lee): The other hardwood valued by the ruling elite, it belongs to the rosewood family and originally came from the south China island of Hainan. Furniture makers often died *huanghuali* to look like *zitan*, but it became so popular among Western collectors that in the late 19th and 20th centuries, the color was often stripped off. Usually thought to have a honey colored hue and a tight, even grain, it can actually range in color from light brown to mahogany dark. *Huanghuali* was long thought to be, like *zitan*, extinct, and finding a *huanghuali* piece of furniture was considered a virtual guarantee of age. But there have reportedly been new stands of *huanghuali* discovered in southeast Asia, perhaps Vietnam, and contemporary furniture makers are busy churning out fakes. So proceed with caution because *huanghuali* no longer guarantees age and value. Although Western collectors will do back flips to find furniture made from *huanghuali*, there is evidence that also Chinese nobles may have regarded it as a primarily utilitarian, not aesthetic, building material.

Huali (Wah-lee): This is not *huanghuali*, although it is sometimes mistaken for it. *Huali* is usually a light, honey color. It's very pretty, but not rare.

Hongmu (Hong-moo): More commonly called "blackwood," *hongmu* is rare but certainly not uncommon. It is often used for decorative trim on cabinets and can show up in chairs and sometimes on smaller cabinets. Its color is a deep, chocolate brown bordering on black with a small grain. We recently sold a small (33 x 19 x 36 inch) cabinet made of blackwood, and it was one of the most beautiful pieces we've ever had. It's a much more interesting wood, to us, than *huanghuali*.

Jichimu (Gee-chee-moo): If you see this hardwood, you will want it. "Chickenwood" is brown with a vivid grain that resembles the layered feathers of a chicken wing. The Chinese often label a wood for the way it looks, and this is one of the most colorful examples. Chickenwood is rare, gorgeous, and adds considerably to the value of a piece.

Wumu: This is ebony: not especially rare and not especially common in late Qing pieces.

Jumu (Joo-moo): Southern elm, this softwood is the most common wood in late Qing pieces. It helps to know that the Chinese idea of softwood differs from the Western designation. The Chinese softwoods are actually hardwoods in Western terms because they come from deciduous trees, not evergreens such as pine. They are called soft because they are porous enough to hold a color. Southern elm is plentiful in central and southern China, and it has an interesting, rich grain. The shapes in the grain earn it the nickname of "pagoda wood." Usually a medium brown color, it can also be light or dark brown. The grain, texture, and coloring are often not especially interesting in bare-wood condition but develop a rich, warm patina with the addition of finishes such as varnish, shellac, and clear Chinese lacquer.

Yumu (Yoo-moo): This is northern elm and similar to *jumu*, the southern elm.

Hetaomu (Het-o-moo): This Chinese walnut is similar to Western walnut in appearance, and its color can range from a medium to dark brown. It is somewhat rare and seems to show up most often in tables from the 18th century. It adds value to a piece.

Huamu (Wah-moo): Burlwood presents an interesting but somewhat academic problem among Chinese woods because its name stems from the appearance of the grain, not the tree it comes from. A burled grain can come from any of a number of woods – maple, walnut, elm, camphor – but the Chinese don't make that distinction. It is thought that Chinese burlwood usually comes from camphor wood (*zhangmu*), but, as we said, it's largely academic. Burlwood is often used as a decorative inset for table or door panels. Burlwood furniture was rare until 1999, when it started to show up increasingly. It's a great touch and adds a nice element of color and grain contrast in the furniture.

Huangyanmu (Wong-yahn-moo): Boxwood is a brown hardwood used ornamentally in Chinese furniture. It grows slowly and produces a trunk that might be 4 inches in diameter at maturity, so it's not practical for furniture panels. But it does hold up well to carving, so you might see it used as relief sculpture on a cabinet or as a carved wooden hinge on a cabinet door.

Baimu (Bye-moo): This is cypress, a softwood, that one sometimes sees in large pieces of furniture, but the light-colored grain is not as imaginative as some of the other woods. It can also be found as decorative trim, since its color blends well with southern elm.

Namu This softwood is similar to cedar and doesn't show up very often in late Qing furniture.

Songmu Songmu is pine, and it is sometimes used for table tops, notably on bamboo tables, and occasionally for entire pieces of furniture. But it doesn't hold up as well as jumu, southern elm, and was not as widely available. The grain is also not as distinctive as jumu, so furniture makers generally did not favor it.

BIBLIOGRAPHY

Berliner, Nancy. *Beyond the Screen: Chinese Furniture of the 16th and 17th Centuries.* Boston: Museum of Fine Arts, 1996.

Berliner, Nancy, and Susan Handler. *Friends of the House: Furniture from China's Towns & Villages.* Salem, Massachusetts: Peabody Essex Museum, 1996.

Clunas, Craig. *Chinese Furniture.* London: Bamboo Publishing Ltd., 1988.

Ellsworth, Robert Hatfield. *Chinese Furniture; Hardwood Examples of the Ming and Early Qing Dynasties.* Hong Kong: Magnum (Offset) Printing Co. Ltd.

Fairbank, John King. *China: A New History.* Cambridge, Massachusetts, London: The Belknap Press of Harvard University Press, 1994.

Kai-Yin Lo. *Classical and Vernacular Chinese Furniture in the Living Environment.* Hong Kong: Yungmingtang, 1998.

_____. *Living Heritage; Vernacular Environment in China.* Hong Kong: Yungmingtang, 1999.

Kates, George N. *Chinese Household Furniture.* New York: Dover Publications Inc., 1948.

Spence, Jonathan D. *The Continent of the Great Chan; China in Western Minds.* New York & London: W. W. Norton & Co., 1998

_____. *In Search of Modern China.* New York & London: W. W. Norton & Co., 1990.

Wang Shixiang. *Classic Chinese Furniture; Ming and Early Qing Dynasties.* Beijing: Joint Publishing Co. Ltd. and Cultural Relics Publishing House, 1990.

_____. *Connoisseurship of Chinese Furniture; Ming and Early Qing Dynasties, Volumes I & II.* Hong Kong: Joint Publishing Co. Ltd., 1990.